Aidan Smith is the author of three previous books: *Persevered*, *Heartfelt* and *Union Jock*. He is a journalist with *The Scotsman* and a seven-times winner in the Scottish Press Awards. He lives in Edinburgh with his wife and four children.

For Stella

BRING ME THE
SPORTS JACKET
OF ARTHUR
MONTFORD

AN ADVENTURE
THROUGH SCOTTISH FOOTBALL

AIDAN SMITH

First published in 2022 by
Arena, an imprint of
Birlinn Ltd
West Newington House
10 Newington Road
Edinburgh
EH9 1QS

www.birlinn.co.uk

ISBN 978 1 90971 556 1

British Library Cataloguing in Publication Data
A catalogue record for this book is available
from the British Library.

Typeset by Mark Blackadder

Printed and bound by Grafica Veneta

CONTENTS

INTRODUCTION

It's an everyday story of media monsters. It's the furthest TV's depiction of family has travelled from Walton's Mountain. But there's a
moment in the American drama *Succession*, in the eyes of many *the*
show of this age, when youngest son Roman Roy does something
perfectly sweet. Rounding off a visit by the entire clan to his father
Logan's native Scotland, he buys the old man a football club.

Roman: 'The Hearts, Dad, it's your team.'

Logan, simmering with dynastic disappointment like he's done
a thousand times before: 'I'm Hibs.'

Roman: 'Hibs? You sure? I thought you were Hearts.'

Logan, about to spontaneously combust: 'Uh, maybe you're
right. How would I know what team I supported ALL MY FUCKIN'
LIFE?'

Still, it's the thought that counts, yes? And would you just look
at Scottish football, getting itself namechecked in such hip and
zeitgeisty circles. And what is it Roman says, wandering into a pub
in Dundee and seeing a match in progress on TV? 'Scottish kicky-
ball. Looks like two eunuchs trying to fuck a letter box. Do some
magic!'

Well, let's ignore that. Just like we'll ignore those English news-

papers and periodicals which every now and again despatch a journalist to 'investigate' our kicky-ball, and on the fastest train out of
Glasgow's Central Station this fearless truth-seeker will report back
that it's 'uncompetitive' because almost without fail the same teams
win.

Although it should be admitted that one such thesis partly
inspired this book. For a brief moment doubt stirred. Had I spent –
gulp, wasted – more than half a century being obsessed with eunuchs
and letter boxes? ...

This isn't a history of Scottish football and, regarding the title,
I'm not putting out a contract on Arthur Montford's blazer with its
unerringly right-angled checks and nor do I covet it. Rather, I want
it saved for the nation in a museum display next to Archie Macpherson's sheepskin.

The book is not an odyssey but hopefully not an idiocy either. I
don't want to call it a journey because everybody's on one of them
right now, so: more of a dauner.

Along the way, from Alloa to Albania, from Brechin's hedge to
Gullane's sand dunes, the aim is to shine an army surplus field torch,
or at the very least an indoor fireworks sparkler, on some of the
moments when Scottish football has been quirky, questing, bold,
different, special, scallywagish, eccentric, crafty and – yes – beautiful
and – of course – daft as a bottle of crisps.

Food is mentioned a lot. Oh, and bevvy. If a psychoanalyst were
to lie me down on the couch then, mere minutes into the highly
expensive session, he might aver: 'You don't actually like football, do
you? When you were young, going to games, you were preoccupied
with the eating and drinking happening around you and the half-
time scoreboard and how funny Tiny Wharton looked in shorts.

'Now, you're obsessed with players who are birdwatchers, players
who read books, players who are politically minded, players who
became teachers and were more fulfilled, players who boycotted
World Cup finals because they couldn't bear the thought of the
ancient rivals winning, players who sold ice cream on the side, from

the side window, players who gave it all up for erotic art, players who romanced pop sex bombs. I mean, do you even know how many times you mention music in the book?'

Okay, but is that not all of us?

Some of these musings date from my first-ever match – 19 August 1967, old League Cup sections, Hibs 3 Clyde 1 – and, hooked for life, the games which quickly followed. (But not that quickly. I hang around the 1970s quite a lot.) Others come from interviews with footballers, usually retired so they can't do anything about perceived present-day ills, but they were characters when they played and remain so in their reminiscences, free from the media training which produces such anodyne guff now.

There are quite a few goalies in the book, perhaps a subconscious riposte to critics and comedians who insist we can't produce any good ones. One thing we can produce is the small but perfectly formed midfielder. We used to be as renowned for bauchly playmakers as we were big ships and some of John McGinn's progenitors are celebrated here.

Am I over the top – a bit prog rock – in some of my enthusiasms? Quite possibly. Is there a running theme? Try as I might, I can't think of a single thing which connects Scarlett Johansson to East Fife. But if I have randomly stitched together what might be called a Bayview Tapestry of personalities and incidents, then one word pops up regularly: indomitable.

It may have been overused but regarding my cast – the nae-luck custodians, the nae-hair inside-forwards, the nae-seamanship winger (nae prizes for guessing his identity), the fans in desperate need of a goal or an upturn in fortune or just a drink, the games which changed minds and saved lives – indomitable just seemed the best fit. The *Oxford Dictionary* meaning is 'impossible to subdue or defeat'. Impossible, too, in the case of these guys, to show themselves to be anything other than 100 per cent Scottish.

There isn't a chapter on Real Madrid 7 Eintracht Frankfurt 3; instead, there's one about the black sheep of our Hampden showpieces, the European Cup final of 1976. No chapters either on Kenny Dalglish or the Lisbon Lions or other Euro winners. No offence, legends, but your stories don't want for exposure and celebration, and instead, for a change, some other characters get a look-in. Call this wilful perversity, call it snatching defeat from the jaws of victory, but what are these if not certifiable Scottish traits?

Oh, and one last thing, Roman Roy: our football contains plenty of magic. Always has done, always will.

1

'The strolling narrator
of the dark blue saga'

ARTHUR MONTFORD:
HOW IT ALL BEGAN

The Yankee Clipper. For years this child's sledge had fascinated me, and given that a sled was the great quest in *Citizen Kane*, the greatest movie ever made, you could almost say it was my Rosebud.

But the Yankee Clipper didn't belong to me, it was Arthur Montford's, and the day when I could quiz him about the precious plaything had finally arrived. 'Sen-say-shun!' as our man would have it.

This was the most poignant of tales, which began some years before with an anonymous 'Wanted' notice in the newspaper small ads. The appeal was spotted by a keen-eyed journalist who turned it into a yarn telling how Montford was trying to source a substitute for the toboggan he cherished as a boy. His marriage had recently broken up and he wanted to be able to pass it on to the grandchildren.

But the search wasn't going well, conjuring up sad images of Montford trudging round junk shops, perpetually disappointed. Here was a man we all cared deeply about: the Voice of Fitba, the commentator-fan, the strolling narrator of the dark blue saga, elucidating mournful laments of non-qualification on repeat, so he had suffered plenty already.

Really, my Rosebud was getting to meet Montford, not long

before he died in 2014. Apart from Dan Rowan and Dick Martin from *Laugh-In* and Fyfe Robertson and Alan Whicker and James Burke from the Moon missions and, okay, quite a number of cathode-ray colossi including of course Arthur's friendly rival Archie Macpherson, I can't think of anyone beyond family who was more present in my life and more comforting, especially on a dank, dead Sunday afternoon.

Our get-together took place at Glasgow Golf Club where Montford was a member. By then quite frail, he asked if I could help him off with his jacket. But the mind was still sharp. And the jacket was still a cracker.

'Fancy you remembering the sledge,' he said. 'It was given to me by my father who was against bicycles which he thought were far too dangerous. It was a rare thing, American-made with proper steering – the front third moved – and underneath I'd painted the name of my father's ship during the war: *Eglinton*. Unfortunately, in the melee that followed the divorce, two items disappeared which I'd dearly wanted to keep. One was my stamp album and the other was the Yankee Clipper.'

'Melee'. That's an interesting word, and especially when recited in Montford's educated, kindly tones, but notice how he didn't use 'stramash'. I hesitate to call this his catchphrase. If he had been an oleaginous frontman for an American game show rather than the host of *Scotsport*, he'd have been blurting 'Stramash!' during every state fair opening, demented grin to the fore, and handing out calling cards with 'Stramash!' in zazzy comic-strip lettering. And the jacket would have been superseded by an exaggerated version of his famous checks, bigging up his celebrity.

Was Arthur without ego? Surely that's impossible in TV. Well, maybe he pulled this off. Maybe he didn't throw a temper-tantrum when the can of film containing the only goal of a dreich game got lost down a well or was flattened by an errant road compressor of the kind always being reported stolen on *Crime Desk*.* Hissy fits didn't sound like Arthur, did they? This sounded more like him, keeping impeccably cool in the face of a fire in the STV studio, just out of shot: '... Greyhound racing now, and it's the Scottish Derby in three weeks' time. I hear there's a very good dog in Bothwell ...'

Or this from commentary: 'And Denis Law implores the ballboy – quite correctly in my view – to carry out his duties a little bit quicker.' The lad was dithering, with Montford regarding it as his duty to ensure propriety for any grannies watching, hoping they couldn't lip-read the Lawman's actual instruction: 'Gie us the fuckin' ball, ya wee basket!'

The two most famous greetings on Caledonia TV are Andy Stewart on *The White Heather Club* warbling, 'Come in, come in, it's good to see you ...' and Arthur's 'Good afternoon, and a very warm welcome to *Scotsport* ...' But only one of them didn't presage dreadful heedrum-hodrum where diminutive gas board clerks prancing in patent-leather pumps were semi-asphyxiated in the Dunlopillo bosoms of stout women wearing tartan tents.

I have brought along a book for Montford to sign. *The Scotsport Football Annual*, 1965 edition. With the possible exception of issue No. 5 of *The Beatles Monthly*, long since lost, this publication says more about me than anything in my possession. It says: 'I love Scottish football, loved it most when Arthur was keeper of the gallery.'

Regarding the sledge, he may have been surprised by my recall but such was the power he wielded across 2,000 editions of *Scotsport*, albeit benignly. Those jacket checks were hypnotic. If you didn't quickly adjust the contrast button on your TV – ask your dad what one of them was – you could end up falling under his spell and following him anywhere. (Most likely, this would be anywhere his beloved Morton were playing, and if not them then the reserves.)

---

* Scottish Television's second-greatest contribution to the tartan telly tapestry, a round-up of thefts and coshings from a real polisman, Bill Knox, stern of sermon and bristling of braid, as he issued what seemed like the same description of the suspects every time: bunch of toerags, brown anoraks. Not a smart sports jacket among them.

Any appraisal of Arthur will always require Archie's presence. In the style of those battle-of-the-bands face-offs – Beatles vs Stones or, more relevantly for my peer group, David Bowie vs Roxy Music – we wondered if the world could be divided up into Montford-ites and Macpherson-aholics. Then we quickly realised this was a spurious argument for we loved them both. Archie on BBC Scotland's *Sportscene* sometimes liked to pronounce or strive for lyricism; Arthur was more couthie. In our abiding image of Archie he's standing – indeed, bestriding – a scaffolding gantry, tarpaulin flapping and seagulls dive-bombing as he delivers his Cronkite-ian postscripts. Arthur on the other hand we always see behind his desk, like he's manning the counter of a well-stocked hardware store, a genial smile inviting us to help ourselves to 15 raggedy minutes of St Johnstone vs Clyde enacted in a Muirton monsoon. Yes, the love was strong.

And these two loved, or certainly liked and unquestionably respected, each other. In England, David Coleman may have been haughty towards Barry Davies who was envious of John Motson being awarded more cup finals than him, but Arthur didn't stick pins in a tiny effigy of Archie nor vice versa.

The great, lost marketing opportunity – doll replicas with teeny-tiny microphones and teeny-tiny clothes rails of stout commentary clobber?

Not required. One set of highlights per show was all that was needed from this Bing 'n' Bob-style double act, stars of the long-running feature, *Road to Dreamland*.*

Any more than that would have been the kind of decadence that causes empires to crumble. None of us demanded every match covered from every conceivable angle, then over-analysed by man-spreading ex-pros in too-tight trousers. If the action disappeared behind a Rugby Park pillar, as it always did, then Arthur could tell

---

* David Coleman, 1978 World Cup, commentating on Archie Gemmill putting Scotland 3–1 up against the Netherlands: 'A brilliant individual goal by this hard little professional has put Scotland in Dreamland.' (See chapter 46)

us what was going on. If Gordon McQueen on Scotland duty was dawdling on the ball, as he often was, we could trust Arthur to shout: 'Watch your back!' This modest amount of televised football might sound like a deprived existence but it was glorious.

So where did Arthur get that jacket? 'Hector Powe in Gordon Street, Glasgow.' His best-ever goal? 'Joe Jordan's winner in the World Cup qualifier against Czechoslovakia – and do you know he used to play for Morton?' The cruellest game he had to describe was England 9 Scotland 3. His most difficult interviewee was Scot Symon ('A nice man but he always froze'). The greatest-ever Scottish player was Gordon Smith. The interview which got away was the same Smith ('I popped into his post office many times: "Please, Gordon, just a sentence on each of the three clubs where you won championship badges …"'). His biggest blooper was calling Billy Ritchie in the Rangers goal George Niven for 45 mist-shrouded minutes. The most difficult camera position, down near a corner flag, was Third Lanark's Cathkin Park. The coldest eyrie was Tannadice.

The only piece of televisual advice Montford received came from the Canadian-born host of *The Carroll Levis Discoveries Show*, the *Britain's Got Talent* of the 1950s: 'Levis told me: "Be nice to the camera."' And Arthur was.

He was first in front of it on STV's opening night in August 1957. Then, in his test-card tweeds, he brought the excitement of the big match to our living rooms, such as for that best-ever goal: 'Still dangerous … the ball's flicked across … the keeper can't reach it … it's there! Jordan scores! Superb header, the ball's in the net and it's 2–1! Magnificent, Scotland. Magnificent!'

At the end of our chat, I helped him back on with his jacket. What an honour. Arthur never found another Yankee Clipper and sadly we've never found another Arthur.

2

*'The pan loaf-fed,
ginger-haired, bandy-legged
exemplar of Scottish gallusness'*

JIMMY JOHNSTONE
ALL AT SEA

The brochure for the Queens Hotel in Largs describes comfortable rooms with their own TVs, trouser presses and fine views of the islands of Arran, Cumbrae and Bute.

Well, of course this is the vista. As Basil Fawlty once almost spluttered, what would you expect to see out of a hotel window on the Ayrshire coast? Sydney Opera House? The Hanging Gardens of Babylon? Herds of wildebeest sweeping majestically …?

In the early hours of 15 May 1974, however, insomniacs and all-night lovers opening the curtains would have been presented with an astonishing piece of theatre: the pride of the Scotland team standing up in a small boat, waving an oar above his head like a broadsword or medieval banner, serenading the fishes and bound for goodness knows where.

Was Jimmy Johnstone re-enacting, almost to the day of its fourth anniversary, the transatlantic crossing of Thor Heyerdahl by papyrus craft, which itself was a re-enactment of the journeys made by the Egyptians 5,000 years before?

But a far more momentous date was fast approaching – the Scots were playing England at Hampden. So shouldn't the imp imperial of the dark blue right wing have been tucked up in bed?

Yes, Heyerdahl ventured by grass hull and Johnstone's vessel was of more solid construction, but the latter's expedition had its own challenges. Johnstone wasn't a celebrated adventurer like Heyerdahl. He wasn't named after the mighty Norse god who governed thunder and lightning; he was known to one and all as Jinky. While he might have been in possession of oars, there were no rowlocks so piloting the vessel would have been virtually impossible.

Plus, he was well and truly blootered.

The Queens was Scotland's base for the British Home Championship, and after they'd beaten Wales, manager Willie Ormond allowed the players to step out for a few drinks. Ormond was no disciplinarian ogre and, given enough rope, these guys were never going to use it to moor an entire flotilla in neat rows. Thus it was gone 4 a.m. when they emerged from their lock-in, feeling miraculous.

Here the tale gets a bit fuzzy. As the thistle-breasted braves sashayed along the seafront, David Harvey was supposed to have climbed on to the roof of a beach hut and chucked pebbles at the stragglers who included dribble demon Johnstone.

Martin Buchan, though, insisted he threw the stones, along with Donald Ford. You'd have to listen to Buchan's version, not least because this pair of swots would surely have been the most clear-headed in the party. But Ford when I spoke to him couldn't corroborate, couldn't remember a bloody thing.

Did the hail of pellets send Johnstone scurrying towards the upturned boats and that's when his bold plan was devised? Or had Jinky already determined that, with night fast turning into morning, what was really needed was 'a wee sail to clear the heid'? This stacks up. Johnstone's relationship with transport was far from casual. Terrified of flying, he'd try and win two-legged European ties at home for his club Celtic, to perform literally as if his little life depended on it, as this was his best hope of being excused the away match.

In Largs, he thought he'd mustered a willing crew and, after clambering on to the chosen boat, held out a hand for them to come aboard, only for three right feet – among the most cunningly accurate and deadly in British football – to launch him into the estuary solo with a choreographed dunt.

At first Johnstone thought this was a good laugh and played to the gallery on the shore. What song did he sing? Some were sure it was Rod Stewart's 'Sailing', which would have been perfect, but the bombastic ballad wasn't released until the following year. Here I trust the recollection of Buchan, the biggest muso I've met in football, who identified the track as 'The Man Who Sold the World'. And I won't easily forget the Aberdeen and Manchester United defender's impersonation – essentially him mimicking Jinky mimicking Lulu mimicking David Bowie – complete with slinky-vagabond gyrations indicating that the ship's skipper had been standing less than serenely on the bridge.

'Oh no, not me, I never lost control,' goes the song, but Johnstone was being sucked out by the tide. Davie Hay and Erich Schaedler mounted a rescue mission only the dinghy they selected wasn't seaworthy. 'It had so many holes in the bottom the two of them could have had a game of putting,' said Tommy Hutchison.

No longer comical, the situation had become desperate. Johnstone was in trouble. The quintessential tanner ba' tyke, the pan loaf-fed, ginger-haired, bandy-legged exemplar of Scottish gallusness, was about to become the man who fell off the edge of the world. His worried team-mates were roaring at him and the commotion woke local residents who raised the alarm.

The police and coastguard raced to the scene but it was two elderly brothers, John and Tam Halliday, who were the heroes of the hour. With intimate knowledge of the water, or watter, amassed over a life-time's ploutering, they steered their launch at the pimple on the horizon and rescued the lucky mascot of a nation's grand, semi-delu-sional sporting schemes and dreams, the proprietor of JJ's nightspot in swinging, downtown Uddingston, the smallest, funniest Bash Street Kid, roll-neck jersey hiding half his face.

Relieved to see Johnstone back on dry land and quick to throw their team blazers round shivering shoulders, his chums needed less than three seconds to start tormenting him about the likely fallout from the escapade. What would his wife Agnes say? What would Celtic manager Jock Stein, definitely of the disciplinarian school, say? What would the press say?

The first condemnation came in the foyer of the Queens. 'Jinky was still chittering under half a dozen jackets,' said John Blackley. 'And the proprietor was glowering at him. "Jimmy Johnstone," she said. "What disgrace you've brought on your country and this place." Jinky popped his head out and sighed: "Please, Mrs Ganley, haud yer wheesht."'

Maybe compared with his wife, his club boss and the seething moralists of the press box, an inquiry instigated by the meek and mild Ormond should have been the least of Jinky's worries. But wee Willie, who'd summoned the entire squad for a high-noon interrogation, was on the warpath. 'He walked in, face like thunder,' recalled Buchan. 'The room went silent, but Jinky couldn't stand the tension. "Christ, you're giein' me some looks, sir!" he said. Willie said: "Nae bloody wonder!"'

Johnstone was indeed slaughtered in the papers. The Scottish commentators were excoriating; the English ones dubbed him a clown. But he dried himself off, wrung himself out and made himself available for selection. By a curious coincidence Stan Bowles, England's flair-packed flankman, also went missing in the build-up to the game, but he failed to show at Hampden and wouldn't represent his country again. Part-timer.

And Jinky played a blinder. Subjected to his diabolical deedle-dawdle, it was the English defence that bore the groggy green pallor of men tossed and turned by the waves. Then, at the final whistle, the wee man directed his filthiest scowl towards the high press box for having keelhauled him, followed by the 'Get it right up yez' fraternal greeting.

Johnstone and his crew were not just indomitable but unsinkable, and the embarrassment and criticism riled them to great heights. Concluded *The Scotsman*: 'The troubles brought a new spirit of fun to the team so that jokes were perpetrated, even on the field against the English. As skipper [Billy] Bremner threw his hands aloft in ecstasy when the game was won, he shouted: "Now we will all get boats."'

3

'Scarlett Johansson's a Hibby'

THE ULTIMATE
CELEBRITY FAN

Celebrity fans, who needs 'em? They can come to your club only to swan off to the hated rivals the way actors finish with one role and pick up another (Sean Connery did this, going from Celtic to Rangers). They can come to your club as much-loved children's TV presenters only to turn into sex pests. They can embarrass you when they talk about your club, getting basic stuff hopelessly wrong, convincing you they didn't attend the famous cup final and never saw the fabled, quixotic left-winger in the flesh.

But then Scarlett Johansson turns up from absolutely nowhere to express her devotion for Hibernian, and rather than scoff you say: 'Respect. Love your work. Your biff-bang comic-book blockbusters and your languid art-house curios – oh, and your 2014 calendar, November especially. I'm running a bus to Cappielow on Saturday – well, a reconditioned invalid car from the cinder perimeters of yore, to be precise; it'll be snug with only enough room for me and you and your impossible beauty – shall I put your name down?'

Admittedly Johansson expressing her devotion for Hearts might have got me swapping teams, doing a Sean, who as a son of Edinburgh's Fountainbridge really should have been a Jambo himself. But it is with the emerald green that she's smitten. Can't resist a young man in durable, crease-free, quik-dri polyester the colour of a freshly mown park on a season's opening day in a country of high-to-absolutely mingin' average rainfall. As team liveries go, *le couleur vert* is oddly rare and almost exotic. The *couleur*, indeed, of Johansson's eyes.

In her 2013 flick *Under the Skin*, Johansson fancies a Hibs fan so much that she eats him. Well, he gets swallowed up by a treacle sea which she seems to be controlling, like Moses in charge of a municipal swimming pool's wave machine, but this amounts to pretty much the same thing.

Note: this fellow isn't a follower of Barcelona or Real Madrid or Manchester United whose strips are worn around the globe and even in mud-hut villages lacking running water. He isn't a fan of those unlovely English clubs nevertheless able to force a fat foot into the sparkly slipper of Premier League membership guaranteeing endless TV riches. He supports Hibs.

Johansson's character is an extraterrestrial who drives around the West of Scotland in a knackered white van looking for men to seduce. In the original book she butchered and liquidated them into emergency fun-sized meat portions for her starving planet. The movie is slightly less concerned with being a satire on the food industry and slightly more interested in having weird, freaky fun with the idea of otherworldliness.

Underneath the coal-black wig, blood-red lipstick and fake fur, that really is Scarlett Johansson, this world's most desirable woman – Scarlett flippin' Johansson! I know actresses film in some highly unusual places but that really is Glasgow's Argyle Street – the spiritual home of the disposable cigarette-lighter tycoon!

Either you're an alien here or everything feels alien to you. The alien's an alien, obviously, but so is Johansson, A-list glamour puss, when she's surrounded by so many folk in grey jogging bottoms. Real people – real, bag-laden, sad-eyed people – wander into the action, unaware of the cameras hidden in the van's dashboard and sunshades. And some of the blokes are enticed into the jalopy by the sci-fi femme fatale with a contender for the silver screen's all-time greatest chat-up line: 'Can you help me find the M8?' Now, say the actress was recognised by one of the guys: would it feel any less alien to be getting the big come-on from Scarlett Johansson, sexy actress, on a typical Glasgow Tuesday than it would from a murderous visitor from another galaxy? More, I reckon.

A Hibs fan can feel like an alien on a typical Glasgow Saturday. You're penned into the away end of one of the big grounds and everyone spits abuse at you, based on their city's antipathy to your own. Either they'll shout, 'You'll have had your tea ya snobby bastard!' or, in easy-to-follow *Play School* mime, tighten an imaginary tourniquet round an arm and make to inject heroin.

Supporters of these other clubs are simply jealous. Yes, there's been a cold turkey scene played out in a bedroom bedecked in Hibs posters in recent cinematic history, but, come on, the film in question was *Trainspotting*, just about the coolest and cultiest flick of the last 25 years. It definitely wasn't *Love Actually*. When hip moviemakers need a football reference, the Hibees are the go-to club.

For the auteur mixing a palette for his film, the Hibs green is perfect. As we've said, it's far from over-familiar but neither is it wilfully obscure. The chap wearing it can usually be relied upon to supply some doomed romanticism, and a bit of comedy to go with the tragedy – and this was certainly the case when *Under the Skin* was shot.

In football, that was season 2011–12, just as Hibs were about to embark on another quest for the Scottish Cup, a trophy they hadn't won for 110 years. They wouldn't win it that time either; indeed they would lose the final most horribly – 5–1 to their Edinburgh rivals Hearts.

So that's not just any old Hibs strip Johansson's prey is wearing. It's the strip from the worst result in the club's history. The strip that looks like a beach T-shirt, which turned out to be apt, the team performing in the final like they were already on their summer hols – a motley bunch of sullen, risk-averse loan signings for whom a hiding from the internecine nearest and dearest caused little pain, so all the emotional devastation was dumped on the supporters.

Yes, the Scottish football fan is indomitable, but when you follow Hibs, and especially that season, there can only be so much heartache and humiliation the spirit can take. So of course in *Under the Skin* the guy got into the van. Of course he plunged right into the treacle. Of course he signed the release form agreeing that his image could be used in the film next to that of Johansson.

'Release me from any more torture while wearing this shirt,' he probably wailed to himself. 'I'm ready to take my leave of this cruel, cupless world.'* The shirt, though, delivered a towering performance in the movie and afterwards took its rightful place in the great Hollywood dressing-up box alongside John Wayne's eyepatch in *True Grit*, Gene Hackman's pork-pie hat in *The French Connection* and, from *One Million Years B.C.*, Raquel Welch's fur bikini – torn from the hide of a woolly mammoth in disappointingly substantial strips but, hey, let's not be too ungrateful.

* Hibs would finally win the Scottish Cup in 2016.

4

*'Like a magician revealing where he'd
hidden the rabbit, the ace of spades and the
sawn-in-half woman from the audience'*

HOW WE GOT
ROUND PROHIBITION

I was promised a jetpack, a moving walkway, three-course meals in pill form. I sat glued to *Tomorrow's World* and believed that anything was possible and waited for Ronco to bring me all my gadgets and aids to modern living. And, sad to say for a child of the Space Race, I'm mostly still waiting.

But I did once glimpse the coat or jaikit of the future. A garment of multifarious pockets, some small, some long, all concealed. A spy might have worn such a jaikit, and many years later such a jaikit was marketed as the ultimate in long-haul flight wear, complete with inflatable neck pillow. But on this day the pockets were full of just one thing.

The Criminal Justice (Scotland) Act 1980 made it an offence to take alcohol into football grounds. One fan got round the ban by stitching pouches across the insides of his match-day cloak of choice. Probably many did this because the Scottish football supporter is nothing if not indomitable.

The super-resourceful fellow I encountered was a Rangers fan. He stood at the top of the terracing, behind a pie stand, and opened his coat for the benefit of his pals. He was an East End spiv showing off stolen goods, Doctor Who on a guided tour of the Tardis's amazing roominess, a magician revealing where he'd hidden the

rabbit, the ace of spades and the sawn-in-half woman from the audience. The pals gawped at the ingenious lining and the telltale bulges:
beer, whisky, maybe some sherry. Praise be, the man in the amazing
Technicolor booze coat!

A drastic law required such drastic action. Fans had been able to
drink freely at the football and suddenly they couldn't, because of a
restaging of Passchendaele. The Scottish Cup final of 1980 between
Rangers and Celtic ended in a mass punch-up involving rival tribes
on the pitch that Archie Macpherson, as well as the First World War
battle, likened to the movie *Apocalypse Now*.

Margaret Thatcher had only been prime minister for a year but
she knew what she didn't like: football. The legislation was quickly
on to the statute books and unequivocal, spelled out on the backs of
match tickets. The forbidden cans and bottles were labelled 'carriers'.
The connotations with disease, manginess, quarantine and isolation
probably weren't wholly unintentional.

Celtic's George McCluskey scored the winning goal in that final,
a nonchalant flick of the left ankle with his back to goal, diverting a
shot which was trundling wide. Thus he is blamed for the riot, the
ban and, in the immediate aftermath, recession, record unemploy-
ment, the disappearance of Hercules the bear, the disappearance of
the sixpence, Cruise missiles at Greenham Common, Bucks Fizz at
the Eurovision Song Contest and the Iran–Iraq War.

'That's still the goal everyone asks me about,' McCluskey told
me. 'Folk either go: "Did you mean it?" or "You're the guy who
spoiled the fun of Scottish football fans forever!"' After the cup
presentation, McCluskey was cavorting on the park in a three-foot-
high green-and-white hat when a police sergeant urged him to hurry
down the tunnel. '"Why?" I said. "Look behind you." It was like a
battle as Archie said, the kind you get in comics when everyone's
mashed into a giant trundling ball, arms and legs everywhere – and
it was heading straight for me.

'So, aye, I'm the killjoy who stopped the drinking, the biggest
party pooper there's ever been, although I refuse to take absolutely

all of the rap. A while ago I got invited to Perth, Australia, by exiled Celtic supporters and I met this guy who reckoned he started the trouble that day. He ran right up the pitch and annoyed the Rangers fans. He booted a plastic football into the net and they piled on to the park. I said to him: "So were you packed off to Oz for that?"'

Basically, the new act was Prohibition. And just like the United States's alcohol ban of the 1920s, the jaikit and other smuggling techniques were the crafty, gasping responses of a people that couldn't do without its bevvy. In America, booze was concealed in everything from the second gas tanks which started appearing on cars to hollow walking sticks. Football fans had fewer props with which they could reasonably squeeze through turnstiles but they did their damnedest to circumvent the crackdown.

At one point supporters started sooking oranges which hinted at a lifestyle rethink as if suddenly they were about to turn into health nuts. In fact, the fruit had been syringed with vodka. Hollywood hellraiser Errol Flynn used to pull that stunt to allow him to continue glugging on set. And W.C. Fields, if he'd been around in 1980, would definitely have raised a glass to our desperate men, who have been too protective of Scottish football to ever claim the alcohol was medicinal because the games could be a tough watch.

Filming his comedies, Fields was rarely without a vacuum flask which he filled with gin martinis and called his lemonade. Once, a practical joker replaced the contents with a soft drink, prompting the furious cry: 'Who put lemonade in my lemonade?'

When Prohibition began, Fields hid thousands of bottles in his attic. Even when it ended he continued to top up his emergency stash, telling Harpo Marx: 'Never know when the darn thing might return, my boy.' In Scotland, though, football remains desert dry. The interdict has been in existence for three times as long as Prohibition and there seems little prospect of it being lifted. So at games you might see straight arms being raised, and wonder what the other arms are doing behind them. A Scottish football fan's desire to drink can encompass the future and also old Eric Morecambe sight gags.

5

'The featherweight nation with the massive and furious pride'

HOW WE ENDURED THE ALBANIAN SOUP AND GOT OUT WITH BEARDS INTACT

We lie about our first time. For instance, first album bought and owned. We'll claim it was something impossibly hip and incredibly dangerous like the Velvet Underground's debut when the truth was more prosaic: *Everything's Archie* by the Archies, purchased from Woolies with a record token, the prize for the best Bible reading at Sunday school.

First film as viewed from the cinema stalls? I wish mine had been *Fritz the Cat* or *Bob & Carol & Ted & Alice* or Julie Christie being thrillingly filthy in *Shampoo*, but it was a whole lot more British and a whole lot tamer – the Norman Wisdom comedy *The Square Peg*.

Here was a silly piece of slapstick about a congenital fool who fell over a lot and, thuddingly unhip as the flick was, I forgot all about it. Then Albania crowned Wisdom a national icon and suddenly *The Square Peg* and its gormless star were cast in a new and favourable light.

You wouldn't call Albania hip in its ultra-Commie guise under dictator Enver Hoxha, but I'd been weirdly fascinated by the place during that time, ever since Hibs played there in 1972. It seemed to be a country like nowhere else. A Soviet satellite state and a land of harsh mountains, harsh soups and harsh ideology in the pamphlets.

Closed to tourists and a virtual prison for natives, it was like the planet Zog, the name indeed of an old Albanian king.

None of this was necessarily bad. I was a spy-obsessed kid who was never without his Secret Sam attaché case (hidden gun, concealed camera, periscope for peeking round corners) and later graduated to Len Deighton novels so the deep, closed-off mysteries of Albania were intriguing.

Hibs were experienced travellers – football conquistadors from the very first European Cup – but had never before encountered what their chairman, Tom Hart, called a 'vicious soccer cold war'. There were arguments over the venue for the tie, switched by the hosts at the last minute. There were arguments over the dire state of the pitch which the Scots claimed must have been a tank training field. There was an almighty row over food – Hibs had brought along their own chef but he was banned from entering any kitchens. Would the match even happen? Yes, but constantly throughout, the Albanian national anthem blared from the public address system with its heavy references to 'traitors' and the need to be 'true men'.

Alan Gordon, the Hibs centre-forward, thought he'd been transported back in time. 'It was like the 1950s,' he recalled, this being the era of Wisdom features like *The Square Peg*. 'There were hardly any cars on the roads, mostly ox carts, so you wondered why there were polis on point duty because they had virtually nothing to do. We liked watching when a car did trundle along – there wasn't much else to amuse us on that trip – because the polis would get very agitated and officious. And come to think of it, the roads were pretty wide, as if Albania had been expecting loads of cars, but something had gone wrong somewhere in its history.'

Maybe this was the moment in 1961 when Albania found themselves virtually friendless in the world. Tomatoes seem to have been the flashpoint here. The Soviet Union patronisingly told Albania not to bother forging ahead with bold new initiatives and stick to growing the humble plant with the identity crisis (fruit or veg?). Albania bit back, insisting the Russian Bear was the one with the identity crisis

33

for going soft on Stalinism. The Soviets cut Albania dead. Albania continued to ridicule revisionist Russia and declared themselves the true keepers of the Marxist–Leninist flame, but by then their leaders were shouting into a void, custodians of the most impenetrable country on the planet.

Maybe Hart was suspected of being a stooge for USSR premier Nikita Khrushchev, who'd fired the first insult in 1961, as paranoia was a regulation-issue greatcoat in Albania. Possibly Albanians believed all their critics were working for the Russkies. They adopted Wisdom as a hero for being a little guy standing up to the big bully, just like Albania were doing. The anthem goes: 'Around our flag we stand united, with one wish and one goal.' Six behind from the first leg against Hibs, FC Besa would need more than one goal and could only manage a draw.

Hibs were pioneering but they weren't Scotland's first. Kilmarnock were actually the first British club into Albania in 1965. In the Commie days, Albania would be erratic Euro participants with politically motivated withdrawals resulting in them being banned from competition, but at least Killie got to play 17 Nentori. Or possibly Partizani. There were a number of ringers from the other club in the line-up.

For 18-year-old Tommy McLean this was a first sojourn abroad and a bewildering one: 'We'd just won the league, champions of Scotland, and had been fantasising about trips to Italy, Spain, even England – a bit of glamour. Albania? I'd never heard of the place, couldn't find it in the atlas.

'As soon as our plane touched down there we were bundled into this army-type hut. No one told us what was happening. We were given some food – pretty terrible – but it was all very strange, like we'd entered the country illegally and any minute the spotlights and thumbscrews would be produced. It seemed like hours we were detained there and then eventually we were moved to our hotel. That was basic, really grim, and I think some of us started to pine for the hut.'

Without knowing it, Killie and the visiting teams that came after would have been chaperoned by the Sigurimi, Albania's secret police, although their footwear wasn't so secret. The great Scottish journalist James Cameron, on his own visit in 1963, noted that their government-issue shoes made a 'harsh and penetrating creak with every step'.

Maybe it's good old Scottish dourness and perverseness – having been reared on potted hough, Ivor Cutler's *Life in a Scotch Sitting Room* and the stingy-pink indentations left by a scudded Mitre Mouldmaster – that fired my curiosity about this angry plook of a Balkan province for their awkwardness, backwardness and isolatedness. Cameron called Albania 'the featherweight nation with the massive and furious pride' and what is Scotland but one of them too?

History doesn't show whether potted hough was standard issue in Albania but meat was rationed and so were newspapers (no foreign editions, just those more-Commie-than-Commie pamphlets). So was TV (none in the hotel rooms) and contact with the locals (Albanians weren't allowed to eat with visitors). The Sigurimi were usually at a corner table, checking up, and there was also a crackdown on crossing yourself after all the churches were ordered to close (three years of a punishment) and pornography (the sentence for being in possession of copies of *Men Only* where nympho-sociologist Fiona Richmond shagged whole towns was surely more severe).

You wonder if a Besa fan, admiring of Hibs, offered a compliment – and you hope for his sake he didn't. In the oral history of Hoxha's Albania, Margo Rejmer's *Mud Sweeter Than Honey*, there's the story of a supporter who said something nice about a German player, earning himself two years in jail. He moaned about prison and got another eight.

Also banned: flared trousers, miniskirts, rock music. And hirsuteness. Hair that was one and a half inches long wouldn't get you into the country and beards were similarly outlawed. Danny McGrain sported fine whiskers when he was one of Scotland's greatest players. A bit less strimming and they would have rivalled Gregory Peck's as

Captain Ahab in *Moby-Dick*. In 1979 Celtic ventured to Albania and could have been denied the services of their esteemed skipper. 'There was a rumour I'd be banned from entering the country because of my beard and I almost wished I had been,' McGrain said. 'Every mealtime the same consommé with a raw egg on top. Out on the streets guys holding hands. To us from the west of Scotland that just wisnae right.'

Scottish football reporters were prohibited from travelling to matches so newspapers asked Celtic players and staff to file pieces. The club had chosen not to bring a chef to avoid causing offence like Hibs. The players sneaked tuck into their suitcases, McGrain a pack of gammon and teabags and Tommy Burns a tin of baked beans. George McCluskey remembers McGrain being eyed with suspicion everywhere he went – 'It was like we were caught up in a spy movie,' he said. After another dismal serving of the infernal soup, McCluskey returned to the room he shared with Burns to find his team-mate shovelling beans into his mouth by hand. 'The orange sauce all over his face matched the colour of his hair. "George," he said, "I'm absolutely starving." My wife had packed me a loaf of bread and some corned beef which I gave to Tommy. I could have charged him twenty quid for them but I didn't.'

Like Hibs, Celtic and Killie progressed in their ties, though none of them managed to register a win on Albanian soil, which was doubtless a huge consolation to this thrawn land. And for Hibs the soccer cold war relented to the extent that the players were invited to a post-match reception before embarking on the complicated sequence of flights back to Scotland. 'Funny old place,' reflected Alex Cropley. 'The Albanian government had basically ordered locals to attend the match and I felt sorry for their players, too. Every strip was a different shade of cherry red and the numbers on the back had been crudely painted. But at least they got to become footballers. The government controlled everyone. If you grew up there wanting to be, say, a ballet dancer and you had the talent but there was a shortage of truck drivers, then you drove trucks.'

Celtic during the traditional pennant exchange were handed a book instead of a little flag – the history of Albanian architecture. What a lovely memento, which could only really have been topped by a VHS of *The Square Peg*, dubbed into Albanian.

6

'The greatest crap golfer in the world'

A ROUND WITH DENIS LAW

Disappointingly, the golf course at Chorlton-cum-Hardy, four miles south of Manchester, has not named its holes. Never mind, I can do this ...

No. 1, a 431-yard par 4 – England Expects. No. 2 – Flags Exultant. No. 3 – Jacks Droop. No. 4 – Alf's Grimace. No. 5 – Hurst's First. Can you see where I'm going with this? It's the story of English football's greatest day, 90 minutes told in 18 instalments, from the fervour at kick-off being doused by West Germany's opening goal and so on, all the way through to the run-in on the inward nine which might include Norbert's Jig, Big Jack's Tears (this hole featuring a water hazard) and of course the 18th, It Is Now.

Why would the golfers of Chorlton have wanted to celebrate a football match in this way? Maybe they wouldn't, but I bet an England World Cup triumph today would see the prime minister, especially one anxious to appear less from Eton and more a man of the people, proposing that all government departments be renamed after the white-shirted heroes. Until, that is, it's pointed out to him that the rest of the UK might not go a bundle on his wheeze.

Famously, Denis Law did not go a bundle on the prospect of England winning in 1966. Rather than watch the final on TV on the

afternoon of 30 July he played a round at Chorlton. If the club president and his committee had after all decided to formally commemorate the Three Lions' success – and called other holes Beware The
Ghost (after Martin Peters) and Hooray For Pickles (in honour of the
Jules Rimet Trophy-retrieving mutt, so a dog-leg) – then I hope they
would have acknowledged that not everyone was delirious about it.
Bahramov's Blunder (Tofiq Bahramov was the linesman who thought
the ball crossed the line for England's third goal) is probably too
much to hope for, so how about Denis's Despair?

Law wasn't despairing in the slightest on the day I met him at
another golf club, Northenden where he was a member, across the
Mersey from Chorlton. He was full of fun and asked often: 'How's
Scotland?' I was keen to learn about his feelings in '66 and also subse-
quently, with his pursuit of the dimpled pebble being viewed and
indeed revered as emblematic of Scottish grumpiness towards
England. But first of all, picking up a coin from the gravel outside
the clubhouse, he wanted to 'fess up to a scam.

'I had an old penny which was double-headed,' he explained.
'Coming back from away games with Man U, we used it to decide
who bought the sweets for the train. David Herd always lost.

'An engineer pal of mine made it for me, soldering two heads
together. But then one day it burst open. Rumbled! Thankfully I was
able to turn to my double-tailed penny, stuck together by my pal
from the leftover bits. You see, son, a war baby doesn't waste
anything.'

Law may have contrived his luck in the post-match malarkey, but
on the field he always secured it honestly, the hard way. By diving
headlong into a thicket of stout calves, down among the reinforced
toecaps and the long studs. By standing up to arch-exponents of the
terminate-with-extreme-prejudice tackling waved through by referees
with a shrug. By steepling headers achieved from huge salmon leaps,
still images snapped down in the grass giving the impression he
jumped higher than the 'Edward Wood – Steelworks' sign on the Old
Trafford roof. And if a ball crossed from the wing arrived just behind

him, by improvising most ingeniously. Maybe the invention of the bicycle in 1817 in Germany was a notable advance for mankind, but who was performing bicycle kicks and scoring with them before Denis?

It was ladies' day at Northenden when we met so there were lots of fluttery waves from the old dears, which the Lawman offered right back. He was nattily attired in pressed shirt, corduroys and Italian loafers and would lament how the Turin he visited for old club Torino's centenary had lost some of its elegance: 'Grown men in trainers – it's gone American.' Not that he was always able to dress so smartly.

Born in 1940 in Aberdeen, Law came through 'the classic spartan Scottish upbringing of that period. There were six of us kids, three to a bed, no pyjamas. Clothes were paid for on tick, music was a comb and paper and Christmas was a Dinky car, a tangerine, a packet of Spangles and an uncrackable nut – but the lad next door would have got no more.'

He was 15 when he left for first club Huddersfield Town, 12 hours on the train, for a starting wage of £4. Once he'd paid for his digs he was glad fish suppers could be bought for a couple of shillings because he sent money home. 'Dad was a trawlerman, always at sea, so I never really knew him, which is something I really regretted.'

One thing Law did know: the old man didn't care for football. Which is interesting because on the day we met he too gave a pretty good impression of someone who could take it or leave it, who knew nothing of some Man U dramas unfolding at that very moment and who preferred to spend Saturdays playing with the grandkids rather than receiving the legend's acclaim from Old Trafford's heated VIP seats.

Legend? A player most happy to be known as one would possibly have a well-polished anecdote for an idiosyncrasy like Law's grabbing of the shirt cuffs. He explained: 'I did that because my nose was permanently snottery.' He had 'no idea' where the overhead kicks and diving headers came from. Preferring to talk up the talents of fellow Scots Dave Mackay, Jim Baxter, Billy Bremner and Jimmy Johnstone, he said: 'I was in absolute awe of John White's command of a football. Do you know that he used to wedge an old two bob bit in the grass then chip the ball from 20 yards, knocking it down every time?'

Ah, I said, but could he have hit one of Law's double-headed jobs? The Lawman pressed on with trying to underplay his thrilling contributions, reminding me that football had simply been his escape from hardship and that he never thought deeply about the game. 'I didn't want to hear about tactics, didn't want to know about the opposition. I always hoped Sir Matt [Busby] would be done with his team talk on the Friday so on the Saturday I could have a wee sleep in the changing room and not be disturbed before the game. Paddy [Crerand] would be kicking the walls, George [Best] would be outside, chatting up all the lassies, but I'd like to be lying on a bench with my shirt over my eyes, thinking about absolutely sweet bugger all.'

Legend? 'Son, we guys from the 1960s may be revered but don't forget that right through that decade Scotland never qualified for the World Cup.' Mention of the national team, though, and his eyes started to twinkle. For the first time he was in serious danger of getting sentimental.

'Being picked to play for your country – boy, it was the greatest feeling ever. The first time, I heard it from a Huddersfield news vendor in broad Yorkshire. 'Tha's lakin', lad' meant I was playing. This was against Wales who'd been to a World Cup and reached the quarter-finals. I remember nothing about the game except that my debut goal was a fluke.

'I loved pulling on that beautiful, pure, dark-blue shirt every time but most of all against England. This was the greatest game which as kids we only experienced listening to the radio. To walk out against them at Hampden in front of that vast bank of howling humanity – well, there aren't words to describe my pride. And then to do it again at Wembley, the lair of the enemy! ...'

So, 1966, England were poised for glory under the Twin Towers while the mob over the border most definitely weren't. A self-confessed 'crap golfer' he may have been, but Law that day became Scotland's greatest crap golfer. He was Sean Connery as James Bond taking on not just Goldfinger in the classic fairways duel but Bobby Moore, Ted Heath, Vera Lynn, Arthur Askey, the MCC, the Chelsea Pensioners, all Morris dancers, the compere on *The Good Old Days*, Jimmy Edwards, bird impersonator Percy Edwards, Malcolm Muggeridge, Terry-Thomas, Joe Loss and his Orchestra, Katie Boyle, Dickie Henderson, cricket umpire Dickie Bird, Bernard Levin, Brian Rix, Joyce Grenfell, the Lavender Hill Mob, Bertie Wooster, ventriloquist act Lord Charles and Freddie 'Parrot Face' Davies. This is how his gowfing that day is portrayed: a heroic, howling, glorious one-man act of absolute defiance. And there must be some folk out there, the most excitable of Nationalists, who would dearly love to see the day's scorecard on permanent public display, perhaps alongside the silver-encased heart of Robert the Bruce.

Law couldn't remember what he shot, knew it was 'well over 100', but no longer has the record of the round. The idea that he was Braveheart with a four-iron in place of a broadsword made him smile. 'I was very passionate back then,' he said. 'If England won I knew I would never hear the end of it from Bobby Charlton and especially Nobby Stiles, and I'd already been shunning those buggers for a while.

'Did I want the Germans to win? Well, my father fought in both World Wars and was shot in Italy during the Second, so not really. Either way, I was going to lose, though the real reason I didn't watch the final was because I was still sulking from Scotland not having qualified for the World Cup. Maybe I was hoping for a terrible game and England getting a spawny one-nil with a disputed last-minute penalty, which is not far off what happened, is it?

'And do you know, son, this is the first time I've admitted that.'

7

'Let's see what's going to happen in the next 28 minutes!'

GENTLY, DAVID FRANCEY BLOWS UP THE RADIO

The radio seemed to be shoogling. Was it actually levitating? Would it, any second now, effect a vertical take-off and smash into the clothes pulley? This was my fear. No, this was my devout hope. I wanted to see the au pair jump and yelp – yes, we had one of those and, yes, she was Swedish – just like happened when the treacle pudding blew the lid off the pressure cooker.

That would have been thrilling affirmation of the power of radio and of football commentary. I supported neither of the teams involved in the Scottish Cup third-round tie being relayed into the kitchen, but the game had me enraptured. It wasn't the radio that was shaking, it was me, hanging on to David Francey's every word.

The funny thing about that match in 1969, Partick Thistle stirring from 3–1 down against Celtic to force a draw in the final minute, was that I bet if I could find a recording, the modest amount of description would come as a surprise. These days we're used to commentators over-talking, over-egging, over-dramatising, but Francey didn't do any of that. He didn't use 4,000 words when just a handful in clipped, Kelvinside Amateur Dramatic Society tones would suffice.

He didn't screech or hyperventilate or gibber madly. Rather than a cheerleader for football, he was more like a curator. Games were conducted tours around his modest civic gallery, prim and perjink. He conveyed excitement and wonder, but in a polite way. Listeners would be directed to moments of interest and intrigue but were invited to use imagination to create a two-act play in their own heads.

Those you might previously have called fringe performers during the course of a football match are far more conspicuous now. Managers are no longer stuck in dugouts which were once just that – holes in the ground where, squatting half-hidden, the gaffers became gophers – and they like to leap around with jumbo notepads drawing attention to themselves. Referees make sure we notice them with their shiny shirts, careful grooming and tattoos commemorating prestigious appointments. Indulging in bantz with the players, they're like the oldest bloke in a nightclub, desperately trying to keep up and not appear invisible. Then there are stadium announcers with Dave Lee Travis's misplaced sense of his own importance and belief in the power of the sound-wave-travelling word – how it can save the world even if merely confirming the insane man-of-the-match nomination from the drunks in hospitality. And commentators love to talk a good game, also a bad game. They'll make a bad one sound epic and tumultuous and would have listeners believe a goal is imminent all of the time, even when the full-back is fannying around on the far touchline, no more in control of the ball than a toddler stumbling after a soap bubble.

In his modest CV for BBC Scotland in 1952, Francey described himself as 'pretty good at English and football mad' and was hired after a 30-second audition. He never encouraged us to think he liked the sound of his own voice, even though it was a fine baritone: mellifluous, vowels as well turned as the feet of an Edwardian occasional table. A voice ideal for ordering a martini, having arrived at the wing-ding by Triumph Stag, but nevertheless one you could trust.

And one you could imitate. Every schoolboy and every pro footballer could mimic him, as could every Beeb colleague, judging by the fact that during an in-house impersonation contest a recording of the real Francey was slipped into the mix and only came fourth.

Imagine a commentator from right now telling the story of Scottish football's greatest day, Celtic winning the European Cup. There would probably be lots of references to the team 'feeling the hands of history on their shoulders', Tony Blair having long since squeezed any remaining potency from that phrase through overuse. Or there might be some over-straining in search of the perfect line only to muck it up, like Oasis did with the album title *Standing on the Shoulder of Giants* – as if the commentator had stood on the *shoulders* of the librarian and pulled out the wrong book.

In Lisbon in 1967 it looked for a long time like Celtic were going to be thwarted by the dull *catenaccio* of the handsome, cologned, international playboy-esque Inter Milan, all dusky, rippling thighs and sparkling teeth. The peely-wally Celts, not so much men of the world but blokes from a ten-mile radius round Parkhead,* had a goalie who kept his wallies in his bunnet. But then: 'A great shot, a great goal by Tommy Gemmell! Tommy Gemmell has scored!' This was how Francey described the thunderous equaliser, and then, composing himself, he said: 'Let's see what's going to happen in the next 28 minutes or so ...'

When Hearts blew the Premier Division title in the final seven minutes of season 1985–86 at Dens Park, here's what Francey said: nothing. Instead, he let the crowd sum up the moment. He knew an almighty and ecstatic Jambo roar had been anticipated, Hearts only requiring a point for the flag, after all. Instead, the noise was made by Dundee fans: innocently old-fashioned gasps of shock and awe. It was as if a busload of bumpkins on an outing to a music hall had been hypnotised into stumbling around the stage by the local illusionist, which was kind of the trick Albert Kidd pulled on the Hearts defence.

Despite being a modest, self-effacing fellow, Francey attracted a few myths. Did he once accidentally swear on air? I'm not sure I want to believe this. Pondering the identity of a Romanian player, legend

---

* All but two of the Lisbon Lions were born within ten miles of the Celtic stadium.

has it he mistook his summariser's exasperation over the name for confirmation of it: 'The big blond striker ... Fuktifano.' Francey's catchphrase was supposed to be 'Oh dear, oh dear, oh dear' but rather like 'We are not amused' and 'Me Tarzan, you Jane' and 'Beam me up, Scottie' he may not actually have uttered the words.

Francey liked radio being called 'the theatre of the mind'. When did that phrase originate? Perhaps after Orson Welles's famous 1938 broadcast of *The War of the Worlds*, which was all too realistic for some listeners, prompting panic about an alien attack. Francey was more concerned with Kilmarnock attacks and St Mirren attacks but he could still conjure up colour and drama and suspense and, maybe most importantly, community – although he would insist it was the football that did this, not him. In his theatre he was quite happy to stand in the wings, a dapper prompt.

We only found out how dapper – snazzy sports jacket, wavy hair – with the first published images of the man at the mic. For my generation, discovering what Francey looked like was the age of celebrity getting properly under way. (For a later generation, this would be signified by Madonna's coffee table book *Sex* and finding out what the Queen of Pop's vagina looked like.)

We were young enough to regard the radio as a mystical object but didn't think that Francey lived inside it. We weren't daft; we knew the radio was where wee Jimmy Clitheroe lived.

Maybe Francey resided in a radiogram; these things were plenty big enough. Auntie Jean had one – a brute of imitation teak and hot valves. As the 1960s started to swing and everyone swapped over to Dansettes and organised orgies round them, hers stood firm against the rapidly advancing grooviness. Always in the corner, always with a starched doily on top, always with the entire clan gathered round like *The Broons*, always with meat paste sandwiches on the go.

And always with Francey at the football: 'Here we are at Broomfield, Stein has centred the ball and it'll be Rangers to kick off ...'

8

'Who's that with Davie Robb?'
(Oh, just Cruyff, Beckenbauer, Pelé ...)

CONFESSIONS OF A
BROUGHTY FERRY SCALLYWAG

Picture the scene as America attempts to sell our 'soccer' to its people. There's Franz Beckenbauer, there's Johan Cruyff and, ah yes, there's Pelé. The game doesn't have any more stardust-flecked names than these three to throw at this marketing conundrum and our heavenly trio are right in the thick of a glitzy schmoozefest in New York, rock stars and the beautiful people gathered all around.

But who's that alongside them, wide of lapel and wild of hair, moustache drooping, merry mayhem in his eyes? Shouldn't someone call security? ...

Then, for the benefit of the celebs, Beckenbauer does the introductions: 'Johan, Pelé, David ...' *David*? That looks a lot like Davie Robb, as we knew him, though the mouser is hypnotic and almost alive and Davie Van Cleef would suit him better. Then the footballers break off from promotional duties and move towards the bar. Robb wants to take the order for drinks but Pelé says: 'No, no, David, you got the last round. What would you like, my friend?'

This was the sweet democracy of the North American Soccer League. We all knew that Edson Arantes was bigger than Oor Davie, one-time thundering and sometime blundering frontman for Aberdeen, but the States didn't. To those lured along to the new sport in town, no one out on the pitch was more famous than anyone else and the World Cup winners among the league's imports didn't seem to mind that. Truly that night and that moment of recognition from the world's greatest – *No, no, David, you got the last round* – was the Scottish game's apotheosis.

'Howzit gaun?' would be Robb's greeting to the glittering assembly. 'Howzit gaun?' he rasped, looking like a ruddy-faced tattie farmer – indeed, like a Kerr's Pink – when we met in a Granite City bistro. 'I live in Banchory, which is 17.22 miles from Aberdeen – or thereabouts,' he explained. A bit of a comedian with a droll Chic Murray-style delivery, he'd muse on the high preponderance of crimpers in his town: 'Do you know that women – that's the opposite sex from ours – will pay upwards of £50 for a haircut?' He was fond of surreal asides; for instance, while the name 'J.R.P. Gordon' for you and me is incomplete without the addition of 'Newport-on-Tay', this being always how the referee was addressed by TV commentators and match programme editors, Robb offered up: 'Weirdly long fingers, rode on Celtic supporters' buses, worked in marmalade.'

I can easily see how this man charmed the NASL and the shipped-in A-listers who glammed up the games. Robb came to them in 1977 after 11 years as a Dandy Don culminating in a League Cup-winning goal against Celtic, although he plays down this achievement. 'I had no ball skill, was useless at heading and just ran about making a nuisance of myself. I played in the shadow of Joseph Harper, as I knew him, the wee dumpling hero of the Beach End. I was once voted Goal of the Season by Graeme Souness on *Sportscene*, wrote a letter thanking him but the bastard never replied. I liked a smoke before games and usually found a guy in the other team with whom I could puff away in the tunnel, then pop our stubbies on a shelf for later. I was a substitute for the final so that might have been a three-fag day. We weren't playing well, and when I was told to get ready, said: "What the fuck do you expect me to do?" But I managed to score a really ugly goal – the most beautiful of my career.'

First for the Tampa Bay Rowdies, then Philadelphia Fury,

Vancouver Whitecaps and Tulsa Rednecks, Robb and the others at the stubby end of their time in the game were encouraged to see and be seen with showbizzers, turn up for parties, dispense guest-list invites to games for the upstart rival to baseball and gridiron and generally spread the gospel.

'Other guys from abroad were Johan Neeskens, Giorgio Chinaglia and of course George Best. I think I might have been introduced to an American crowd the first time – and usually they numbered 70,000 – as the bloke who'd won the "Scotch League Playoff Cup". But who was to know that wasn't any less of a trophy than the World Cup?

'Those parties were amazing. Well, apart from the one where everyone had to deposit their guns on the table – that was alarming. There was dinner with Frank Sinatra. I had to deliberately cut myself shaving the morning after to make sure I was still alive. I was introduced to the crowd at a Harlem Globetrotters match. Dave Gilmour of Pink Floyd became a friend. I went on stage with the band Yes and mucked about on bass guitar. Can you honestly imagine all of that happening to a boy from Broughty Ferry?'

Another surely-must-wake-up-soon moment: sitting in a Jacuzzi full of vodka with Rodney Marsh. 'Rodders became my big mate out in the States. He was in demand as a model. I did a bit too but he was much prettier. And a trendsetter. Once he turned up for a job in a T-shirt that read 'Fuck you'. The sponsors told him he couldn't wear it so he cut out the sweary word and that started a trend of fans with holes in their clothes.

'Another example of his power and influence: for a laugh he filled out this questionnaire with Smirnoff vodka in every answer – Q: "Who would you most like to meet?" A: "The guy who makes Smirnoff vodka" – and the guy who did was so delighted he sent Rodders a lorryload of the stuff, 144 cases. They completely filled his garage. He was giving whole boxes away. Then he poured a load of it in his Jacuzzi.'

Robb had countless stories like that and warned me that some would stretch credulity.* 'A lot of footballers embellish, maybe to come across as the big man. Or perhaps they're not meaning to tell lies as such but the truth gets lost. Well, I'm David Robb and one night in New York there was this stunning girl. Our eyes met across a crowded room, as the saying goes. This was Sammy Davis Jr's penthouse and everyone was gathered round the piano while he played. The girl and I got talking. I had no flippin' idea who Olivia Newton-John was. She came to the Rowdies' next game in Buffalo and then back in New York she invited me to what I thought was going to be a party at her apartment overlooking Central Park but I was the only person there. One thing led to another ...'

One fling led to another, too, when later on this fantastical voyage Robb found himself backstage after a Fleetwood Mac gig: 'I knew who Stevie Nicks was. Everyone was drinking and drugging – well, the band were on the drugs. Stevie asked me where I was from. 'Scotland – it's a little village outside London.' She seemed to like my crap jokes, and to be just as keen as me on doing a runner from the meet-and-greet. We popped into a nightclub – I remember she didn't have any money so I signed the bill in the name of a club director – and then it was back to her hotel. Ach, everything was so free and easy. It was great ...'

Davie Robb, friend of the stars, football frontiersman and another example of our indomitability.

---

* When Davie Robb died in July 2022 it was impossible not to think back to the last words he said to me, just as I was boarding my train out of Aberdeen. He was still reflecting on the 'fantastic' US years. 'So free and easy,' he repeated, as his features reddened some more and formed into a mischievous smile. 'And there was something else ...' As I was completing the book, I tried to get back in touch so he might elaborate on this final reveal, hitherto unpublished, but my attempts failed. At the start of our chat, he'd admitted: 'Some of the stuff that happened to me I'd have terrible trouble getting anyone to believe.' There was something else – there was *someone* else. Another fair and famous maiden who'd fallen for his rough charms. He said, 'You're the only person who knows ... Princess Caroline of Monaco.'

9

'The original home of soccer madness'

OUR GREATEST EUROPEAN FINAL
(IT'S NOT REAL vs EINTRACHT)

Tony Blair had a vision. The Parliamentary report promoting his 24-hour drinking laws promised 'Bologna in Birmingham and Madrid in Manchester'. In 2005 the prime minister wanted to create 'continental café culture' in Britain.

But it didn't quite work out that way. England in particular struggled with the new freedoms. The maypole in sundry towns became a mast with a CCTV camera on top, usually situated near a Wetherspoons, and the wind-tunnel pub chain's clientele would gather round to argue, carouse, steal each other's boyfriends/girlfriends, idiot-dance, fight, fall over and throw up.

When they could find room on the pavements, that is, for right away the best vantage points were commandeered by social anthropologists, Channel 4 documentary makers, Eurotunnel tourists from the continental mainland and why-oh-why? columnists for the *Daily Mail*, all of them keen to be amused and/or appalled by the modern interpretation of Hogarth's Beer Street, complete with hair extensions and happy-slapping.

If only Blair had been in Glasgow on 12 May 1976 when he would have seen the experiment succeed. Gloriously.

For the European Cup final at Hampden between Bayern Munich

and Saint-Étienne, the City Fathers granted 1,000 late licences allowing pubs to stay open until 3 a.m. Now, to those of a glass-half-empty disposition, this seemed like a dangerous cocktail. Not quite in the realm of China taking ownership of the atom bomb – the comparison made by the 1960s London underworld when psycho-hoodlum 'Mad' Frankie Fraser joined a gang of villains already boasting a diabolical reputation – but not far off. Hard-drinking Glesca, though, played a blinder.

Glasgow wasn't violent, it was vivacious, and especially its womenfolk. *The Scotsman* reported the continuation of an age-old welcome from the little old ladies of the Maryhill district – beetling down to the city centre to press boiled sweets in the hands of the visitors. Meanwhile the younger set – wee hairies and glam-rock bauchles – applied lipstick of a shade you'd have to call 'Midnight on Sauchiehall Street' and went all out to win the European Cup of snogging strangers.

Most of the recipients of these snogs were French. Why did Glasgow align itself with Saint-Étienne? Because they were the underdogs. They offered musky, musketeery romance. They played football with crazy abandon. They had cool hair. They had a cool strip, even though it was green, even though the blue half of Glasgow – Rangers – had lost to Saint-Étienne earlier in the competition. The team were happy to be in the city; their supporters delighted.

So were the German supporters who enjoyed as much beer and snogging as they would be permitted by their hosts, for Glasgow was well within its rights to be grudgeful towards the Bayern contingent after being slighted by the club's president.

Wilhelm Neudecker tried to persuade European football's governing body, UEFA, to take the final away from the city, claiming the crowd would be embarrassingly low. The inference was that the doltish locals wouldn't know a glamorous sporting showpiece if it hit them on the head. But that's dangerous talk in the home of the Glasgow Kiss (warning: does not contain actual kissing).

Less than thrilled to be on Clydeside, Bayern after the game got the hell out of town as fast as they could. Neudecker had been worried about security, specifically the threat of terrorist action by the far-left militants of Germany's Baader-Meinhof Gang, with the final following in the wake of their co-founder Ulrike Meinhof being found hanged in her prison cell. Glasgow, though, isn't the sort of place to cower from terrorism. In 1977 at the height of the Irish Troubles, a bomb thrown into Derry Treanor's pub, popular with the Catholic community in the Gorbals, was casually kicked back into the street before it exploded. In 2007 at the local airport, baggage handler John Smeaton barred the way for a flaming jeep being driven at the entrance. He booted one of the occupants in the testicles and declared: 'Glasgow doesn't accept this. We'll set aboot ye.'

Neudecker seemed to forget, or maybe didn't know, that Glasgow had already staged the greatest club match of them all: the 1960 European Cup final. He should have known this, given it featured a German team, although most people's abiding memory of Eintracht Frankfurt is their goalie getting lost in the folds of his net while searching for a ball buried at the foot of a stanchion like an unexploded depth charge. Real Madrid won the solid-gold classic 7–3.

As a football spectacle the final of 1976 wasn't in the same league. Saint-Étienne were plucky and unlucky, hitting the woodwork twice,* before a single goal won it for Franz Beckenbauer and Bayern. But for everyone who toasted the match prior to kick-off, and for a long time afterwards in Glasgow's biggest display of exuberance since VE Day, it was unforgettable. Or it would be if only they could remember it.

Now, it would be thrilling to report from the bars that while German men looked on, arms crossed in a stiff, neutered fashion, Scots and French intellectuals in denim jackets hunched round tables

---

* Hampden's goalposts were of the outmoded flat-fronted sort with Saint-Étienne were convinced that the round design would have won them the trophy. Rival fans mocked them over *les poteaux carrés* – the square posts – but the club would later try to buy them from Hampden with the brave intention of confronting their demons.

slooshing with Double Diamond and lobbed existentialist theories at each other. Then, stepping into the chill night air to be reinvigorated by suppers *à les puddings blanc*, that the Auld Alliance then introduced surrealist art to the conversation with the Germans still standing pointedly by, faces absurdly blank as if painted by Magritte.

It might be safer to say that '76 was mostly about the kissing. The boldest girls – those feel-me-up pioneers from the school playgrounds with their feather cuts – were first to engage. They reported back to the others on the merits of 'with tongues aye ye ken' in an EEC context and, while the second wave was in progress, they nipped home to change into shorter skirts and higher heels.

'Where did they all come from?' wondered *The Scotsman*. 'Where had they left their boyfriends? Who told them it would be warm enough for that décolletage?'

Match night in Glasgow in the hooligan-heavy mid-1970s was often a nightmare for the polis, especially at the final whistle with one lot likely to be exceedingly grumpy. Not this time. The beaten Saint-Étienne fans summoned a big, collective Gallic shrug and returned to the Pale Ale howffs where *les demoiselles* were waiting patiently like football widows, there to resume a contest the French were always going to win.

'Cocus!' was the chant they directed at the Germans celebrating victory, meaning that while their opponents might have been lucky in sport, they were unlucky in love.

In a leader column headlined 'Haste ye back', *The Scotsman* of the next day was devastated that 'the extraordinary Glasgow Festival of 1976' was over as the final had given the city back nothing less than its *raison d'être*. The place had been written off, heart ripped out, the people decanted to new towns to make way for motorways. But, said the paper, on the evidence of the past few days and one especially long night, 'the native woodnotes warble sweetly still'.

Glasgow had reclaimed the title of 'the original home of soccer madness'. And sealed it with a kiss.

10

'Don't you remember I awarded you a shy in your own half in the eighth minute?'

TINY WHARTON, GIANT AMONG WHISTLERS

It was 1971 – a big year for the Tinys of the world. Tiny Rowland was engaged in the ruthless business methods which would see him dubbed 'the unacceptable face of capitalism'. Tiny Tim was at the peak of his popularity as the weird ukulele minstrel on *Rowan & Martin's Laugh-In*. Elton John was recording 'Tiny Dancer', the sweetest of all his piano ballads. And Tiny Wharton was refereeing his fourth and last Scottish Cup final.

I first bore witness to the work of Wharton, the greatest Tiny of them all, earlier in that competition in the tie between Hearts and Hibernian. The final wouldn't be a game as much as a conflagration – Celtic vs Rangers – so that Edinburgh derby must have been a stroll in the park for him, or as Tiny Tim would have it, a tiptoe through the tulips.

Tim and Tom, Wharton's real name, shared a colossal build, but there the similarities ended. Wharton in the capital's minor skirmish was more reminiscent of a character from the silent comedies I used to watch on Boxing Day TV: Eric Campbell, Charlie Chaplin's Dunoon-born ogre. In these two-reelers Campbell would invariably stand and roar and flare bushy eyebrows and demand a return to order while everyone else scurried around, crashed into each other and fell over. This was slapstick, which would be a pretty accurate description of Tiny and his match; the only thing missing from the latter was the fast and furious piano.

It was crucial to the hilarity that Campbell was big and plodding but the man probably couldn't have moved any quicker if he'd tried. Wharton was in the same boat or slow-turning tanker so he devised a way of refereeing an entire game from the centre circle. He achieved this through the force of his personality and the power of his glower.

The nefarious footballer might think he'd found the equivalent of a dark alley down by the touchline in which to boot an opponent up the backside – but a glance over his shoulder would tell him that Tiny was all-seeing, and that punishment was quickly coming. In extreme circumstances, Wharton did move. Obviously if brawls broke out involving two entire teams, both dugouts, the macaroon-bar sellers and the half-time scoreboard operator, he would lumber right into the rammy's epicentre.

Tiny wasn't a mute official. He delighted in deadpan drollery, bons mots amid the pell-mell. In delivery terms the actor from Old Hollywood that he most resembled was probably W.C. Fields. Maybe Fields portraying the headmaster of a tumbledown boarding school, or the dean of a corrective institution for unruly boys. Wharton's word was law and yet no player ever spoke of him deriving sadistic pleasure from his iron rule. The witticisms would soften his censures, and the unholy rabble liked that he addressed them as 'Mister'. Falkirk's Doug Baillie was one of many who remarked that it was almost a pleasure being punished by Tiny.

Hearts' Johnny Hamilton was fouling and narking to equal degrees, his complaints a splutter of mumbles as he always played with his false teeth left in a jar back in the dressing room. Eventually Wharton tired of his spittle-flecked moaning. 'Mr Hamilton,' he announced, pointing up the tunnel, 'it's time to be happily reunited with your wallies.'

At the end of an Old Firm game won by Rangers, Celtic's Bertie Auld girned to Wharton about a litany of injustices. 'You big bandit, you gave us nothing today,' he grumbled. 'You're wrong, Mr Auld,' came the retort. 'Don't you remember I awarded you a shy in your own half in the eighth minute?'

Auld, because he appreciated quippery and dealt in it himself, had many such encounters with Wharton. Playing for Birmingham City against Espanyol in the Inter-Cities Fairs Cup with Tiny refereeing, he was urged by his team-mates pre-match to butter up his countryman. 'You and me will be the only Scots on the pitch,' ventured the bold Bertie. Wharton didn't respond until well into the second half when he confirmed there would be no favouritism by dismissing Auld thus: 'Remember when you said there would be only two Scots on the park? Now there's only one. Off you go.'

On another occasion an exasperated Bertie asked our man: 'If I called you a bastard would you send me off?' Wharton: 'Of course I would, Mr Auld.' 'What if I just think you're a bastard?' 'There's nothing in my rulebook which allows me to act on random deducements, unexpressed.' 'Well then, I think you're a bastard right enough.'

Wharton looked highly comical. He was a Brylcreemed behemoth. He was an exceedingly large man in shorts. His socks only made it three-quarters of the way up his peely-wally calves. Unable to find a ref's shirt to fit him, he opted for a blazer. With that big badge on his breast pocket, he was no longer the headmaster but the overgrown sixth-former, a Bunterish prefect.

No one was going to mention, anywhere within earshot, his faintly ridiculous mien although the little guys of Scottish football weren't intimidated by him. Alex Edwards of Dunfermline Athletic felt he wasn't getting enough protection and stated his case forcibly. 'Now, Mr Edwards,' sighed Wharton, 'you'll notice that I stand 6ft 5ins high while you seem to be at least two feet smaller. Please, can you be advised to shut the fuck up?'

Also at Dunfermline, goalkeeper Jim Herriot required physio Jimmy Stevenson after saving a shot with his bollocks. He recalled: 'Standing over me, Tiny said: "Mr Herriot, were you planning to go winching tonight?" "Yes, Tiny." "Then be still while Mr Stevenson administers his tender mercies with the magic sponge and you should be fine for your evening at the *palais de danse*.'"

Pint-sized Tommy McLean of Kilmarnock tried to match his huge stride. 'It's no' fair, it's no' fair,' he groaned. 'What's not fair, Mr McLean?' 'That I have to pay the same as you for a suit.' And Celtic's Jimmy Johnstone became so familiar with Tiny's adjudications that he began to act as the official's comedy 'feed'. 'Name,' demanded Wharton. 'Roy Rogers,' quipped Jinky. 'Well, Mr Rogers, you'll find Trigger waiting for you in the dressing room.'

On one of Wharton's rare trudges he arrived in the penalty box just in time to see the ball bounce over the byline whereupon he awarded a corner. Protests that it should have been a goal kick were met with the rebuke: 'I've just sprinted 50 yards to follow play. If you think I'm going to sprint back another 50 yards to be in position for a goal kick then, gentlemen, you are clearly aff your heids.'

But Tiny could show nimbleness when required. Told by Celtic's Charlie Gallagher he was standing in the way of a free-kick, he quipped: 'You do your job, Mr Gallagher, I'll do mine.' With the ball about to hit him he jumped up in the air, allowing it to reach Bobby Murdoch who scored. 'Thank you, Mr Wharton,' said Gallagher. 'Don't mention it, Mr Gallagher.'

He liked discourse but would always have the last word. John Greig protested that a goal against Rangers was offside. 'That was a terrible decision,' he complained. 'It was a goal, Mr Greig.' This went on for a while until Tiny affirmed: 'Sorry, Mr Greig, but when you collect your *Sunday Post* tomorrow you will see the result in black and white. This should encourage you to accept it was a legitimate score.'

Pat Stanton of Hibernian was irked by the sight of Wharton removing his sharpened pencil from that badged pocket and tried to be clever. 'S-t-a-n-t-o-n,' he offered, Primary 1-style. The booking was immediately upgraded: 'Since we seem to be having a spelling test, Mr Stanton, here's one you might manage: t-a, t-a.'

Very occasionally, a player would fool our pre-eminent adjudicator. Stanton's team-mate at Hibs, Eric Stevenson, squeezed a penalty out of Wharton in a league game at Dundee. Foolishly, he tried his luck back at the same venue a few weeks later in a cup tie, only to be informed: 'Not today, Swan Lake.'

11

'Dive! Dive! Dive!'

ARGENTINA BY SUBMARINE

It's not every day that you google a word, name or phrase and only three suggestions come back. And it's certainly not every day that an enquiry concerning *Doctor Who* produces such a modest return, given all the bampot obsessives in Cyberman cyberspace.

Ah, but this query relates to the old, black-and-white, macho *Doctor Who*, where the cry was always 'Ex-ter-min-ate!' and not 'In-clu-siv-ity!' Where men were men and often ramrod-straight brigadiers and never a wobbly chin was seen. Where the audience for the programme was massive and undemonstrative, not a third of the size and all with their own vlogs. And where spin-off merchandising was a Christmas annual with a fold-out illustration of deal-with-it-kids terror such as the Dalesub.

I thought I'd remembered the term wrongly, given that written down it seems so odd, but here's the confirmation: Dalesub (*Dah-leh-sub*), a submarine piloted by Daleks. Shows I was paying attention all those years ago. Shows that the cutaways in the illustration of key areas of the horror craft such as the periscope gantry and the torpedo chambers – Daleks crammed together in suffocating corridors, metal monsters within a metal monster, all of them desperate to kill – left a lasting impression.

Who would willingly undertake a voyage in a submarine? Can you imagine the hatch shutting with a doomy clunk and a sucking whoosh followed by eerie silence and the only means of egress being available again any time soon? Picture yourself descending the ladder and being greeted by a battery of whirry guns where right arms should be, all pointing directly at you.

Or ... picture yourself descending the ladder and being greeted by a bunch of Scotsmen in kilts.

This didn't scare Jim Tait. In 1978 the Hamilton restaurateur envisaged standing on top of the sub, as he'd seen commanders do in war movies, waves lapping over his feet when he welcomed aboard a rumbustious Tartan Army detachment for a famous expedition to Argentina's World Cup.

It was a bold idea but then typical of a populace that went right ahead and wore the plaid with Adidas Sambas and dirty-white towelling sports socks, many of them purchased three-pair-for-a-pound from vendors in Glasgow's Sauchiehall Street, not caring how ludicrous the combo looked. This was a cheerfully un-self-aware era, some years before the emergence of the hunky, chunky-booted, Braveheart-inspired, bronzer-daubed, gadgie-scaped professional Scotsman. Maybe there had been some naivety and confusion over Argentina's exact position on the map, for this was also a few years before the Falklands War when it became known to everyone. Could a submarine travel all the way down to the South Atlantic without having to refuel? Could one even be chartered for private use? Undaunted, Tait costed the big adventure at £40,000 and was taking names.

All Scotland was giddy with World Cup excitement as the team entered the rarefied realm of sports-celeb endorsement. Ally MacLeod, the hyper-enthusiastic manager, advertised carpets and such was the fervour he'd inspired that probably everyone expected him to fly to Argentina on a magic one. Would his players be going by car? They promoted Chrysler Avengers with the commercial's 'storyline' requiring them to open the drivers' doors in rapid sequence. The synchronised glaikit gawping of Bruce Rioch, Don Masson and the rest made them look like over-keen enlistees at a dogging club – an impressive feat given that, like the Falklands War, vehicle-based voyeurism, watching or participating in bonnet bonking, had yet to be invented.

The Beatles seem to have been submarine enthusiasts. In the film *A Hard Day's Night*, John Lennon was glimpsed in the bath playing with his toy subs and the song 'Yellow Submarine' predicted 'sky of blue, sea of green' every voyage, although the Fab Four may have changed their tune after trying LSD for the first time, the nightmares convincing Lennon he was trapped underwater in a giant cigar case.

H.G. Wells invented the modern world but wanted nothing to do with this diabolical form of transport. While he thought time travel realistic and trips to the moon achievable, he declared: 'I must confess that my imagination refuses to see any sort of submarine doing anything but suffocating its crew and floundering at sea.'

The dream of a sensational World Cup triumph might have overridden any concerns in the fans' minds about making the 11,300-mile journey underwater, but surely they would soon encounter all manner of phobias, collected into an unwelcome pack waiting for them in their bunk rooms. Ipobrichiophobia is a fear of submarines and submechanophobia is a fear of submerged man-made objects. Then, never mind claustrophobia and aquaphobia, there's cleithrophobia (fear of being trapped) and thalassophobia (fear of oceans).

Thalassophobia isn't to be confused with thaasophobia, a fear of boredom. This opens up a whole can of sea worms, including ludophobia – a fear of board games. Surely there's also a fear of quizzes ('Arbroath 36 Bon Accord 0. How many Red Lichties goals were disallowed by the referee?'*) and a fear of the onboard library having nothing left to read apart from Dan Brown.

In neuropsychological theory, a fear of cylindrical objects has been identified but not yet named, possibly because even head

* Seven

doctors who are normally so keen to put a name to every condition, real or imagined, cannot quite believe how many of them can be related to submarines.

I repeat: who in their right mind would submit to a submarine? It would subjugate you, and it wouldn't be sublime or even subliminal. In fact it would be sub-human. Your waking hours would be spent with people you started out thinking were like-minded, your new best friends sporting the same Adidas Sambas, but before long you'd want to kill them and might very well have to end up eating them. Your bunk would feel like being stuck inside a Samsonite suitcase, or an MRI scanner with the grimmest of prognoses, and you wouldn't be able to sleep for thinking about that episode of *The Alfred Hitchcock Hour* when the conman hiding in a coffin six feet under discovers that the accomplice who should be digging him out of the ground so they can claim their booty is alongside him and, what's more, potted heid.

Well, the submarine never went to Argentina. Too scared to have gone, I'm now too scared to find out why the voyage was cancelled, in case it was for a completely mundane reason (is that a recognised phobia?). But I want to believe that Jim Tait and his crew would have been like Lt Werner in *Das Boot*, the greatest submarine movie of them all. A naval journalist, Werner was tasked with recording the 'glory' of life under the waves. 'I want to stand before something relentless,' he declared, as he was about to dive 10,000 leagues. 'Where no woman crosses our path, and no mother looks after us. Where only the reality reigns, cruel and large.'

That was Argentina, all right. Insisting Tait's recruits undergo a cruel and large journey before the cruel and large notoriety of Scotland at the World Cup would have been too sadistic, even by our standards.

12

'*A burr to soothe a growly old dog*'

JAMES ALEXANDER GORDON, RESULTS ROUNDER-UPPER

Saturday, five to five, the classified results on TV and the long wait – the trundling train ride through sundry market towns and other Englandshire places of disinterest – for the Scottish scores. 'League Division Three ... Bristol Rovers 0 Halifax Town 0 ... Chesterfield 0 Port Vale 0 ...'

'Couple of crackers right there,' chuckled my father, as the solemn decree continued: 'Torquay United versus Plymouth Argyle – late kick-off ...'

'No! Again? What's happening down there? It's Torquay, not the Tower of bloody Babel ...'

All home games for this club were the same. After Dad explained his joke – teeming, chaotic, no semblance of order, things we doubted were Torquayesque, although couldn't say for sure – a running gag developed in our house where every second week the aim was to try and outdo each other with ridiculous reasons for a football match being delayed down on the English Riviera. His were inventive, mine were silly (Dad: 'You said "Invasion of giant spiders" last time'), but it was a ritual which soon didn't need there to be a held-up game causing confusion and turned into a form of greeting between us.

Imagine the disappointment, though, when we found out that

Torquay's matches hadn't failed to start on time because of the referee swallowing his whistle or a mass outbreak of streaking or a meteor strike or a centre-circle sit-down protest over proposed changes to bin collection day or the visiting team's bus being hijacked and rerouted to Cuba but had always been scheduled for 7.30 p.m., a club experiment to drum up more support. 'The blithering idiot should have said "evening kick-off" rather than "late",' complained Dad, and having lost faith in the telly announcer, we then switched to radio and James Alexander Gordon.

This was more like it. A voice you could trust, a lilt that might be the secret ingredient in marmalade, a burr to soothe a growly old dog. It would be some years before the BBC would go regional accent-crazy, so this mellifluous Edinburgher was a trailblazer. 'They wanted different voices and hadn't got a Scottish one yet, on the national network,' Gordon said of his appointment, begun with a stint on Radio 4's *Shipping Forecast* which wasn't insignificant.

As announced by him, clubs' names were rendered as windswept and evocative as Fisher, Dogger and German Bight. Dad and I were biased, but those resonating the most were Scottish ones such as Airdrieonians, Heart of Midlothian and Hamilton Academical. Not being able to scan the results like on TV before Gordon arrived at them merely enhanced the recital on Radio 2, adding intrigue. All hopes, dreams and terrors were neatly encased in those few tense seconds. And it was a recital, like he was reading from a musical score rather than a list of football scores.

'I trained as a musician and I think music had a lot to do with the way I delivered the results,' he said. 'All those names … I first looked at them and wondered if, rattled off straight, they might be quite boring. I thought I'd do something different, try and add some drama and maybe a little bit of excitement. I play the piano and the clarinet and decided: "Let's make the results sound like a song."'

Who would have thought the song of Gordon's life would rise to this crescendo? At the peak of his teatime powers he possessed one of the most recognisable voices in the land, and also one of the most reassuring. Counting the clubs in and counting them out, all in their usual places, he was, said Michael Palin, like the medieval crier 'beating the bounds'. Another comedian, Eric Morecambe, held his breath every week hoping Gordon would declare the result of all results: 'East Fife 4 Forfar 5'. But it was a song which had begun so sombrely.

Gordon's mother died in childbirth and he was brought up by adoptive parents. Aged just six months, he contracted polio and was paralysed. For many years he was unable to walk or talk, eventually learning to pronounce words from RAF officers who were recuperating in the same hospital after the Second World War.

Because of his leg irons he couldn't play sport but, encouraged by his parents who refused to mollycoddle him, he'd show great willing, even if it meant standing in as a corner flag, hankie in his mouth, for school football.

During his recuperation his father had wired him up with a steam radio and he was entranced, listening to the Home Service until close-down. Later, as the old man was checking his football pools coupon against the results, Gordon noticed him getting frustrated with them tumbling out of the wireless too quickly. So, despite his speech impediment, he would read them to his dad at a more leisurely pace.

What did Gordon's tough start in life teach him? Maybe empathy. In his trademark cadences he would go up for the winning team – 'I'd smile with my voice because I was pleased for them' – but drop into an expression of sorrow for the beaten side.

The influence of Jimi Hendrix is not apparent but – in common with other characters on these pages – there was a highly improbable encounter with a rock star. In his previous life in music, Gordon was an easy-listening promoter, when who should saunter into his office one day but the guitar god. 'Got any shit, man?' Hendrix enquired. As a cruise ship piano player, Gordon hadn't witnessed too many orgies and there was naivety about drugs. 'I was completely baffled and only found out later what Jimi meant. You see, I was a Condor man.'

It's easy to conjure up an image of James Alexander Gordon puffing on his pipe during the results. Next to him would be a ripping yarn by John Buchan with a page folded at the chase scene, to be reread when he could allow himself to get excited. He'd be looking forward to a G&T with Morecambe in the BBC Club. And if this was to be the Saturday – finally! – of the Fifers-Loons nine-goal thriller, how many times Eric would waggle his specs in delirious acclamation?

But always, before getting to the Scottish scores, he would be confirming beyond all reasonable doubt that those crazy cats down Torquay way were not 'late', but 'evening'.

13

'Long bangers between garage doors under a single, sparking street lamp'

EAST FIFE TRIP THE LIGHT FANTASTIC

I still feel bad about it. Condemning my wee sisters to an afternoon deep in the dark heart of the Fife interior. No offence, Methil, and I'm not calling you a 'dump' as the Duke of Edinburgh was once supposed to have done, but this was January on a public holiday in the early 1970s. You really didn't have a whole lot going for you.

Goodness knows how my mother amused the girls while Dad and I were at the football at the old Bayview, home of East Fife. I've always been afraid to ask what the alternative entertainment might have been. Which vandalised play park they endured until little icicles began to form on pigtails in the perishing cold. Which locked-up cafés forgot to flip the door's 'Open' sign to 'Closed' and, completing the sadistic joke, offered a window display of a three-tier cake stand, bereft of buns, not even a plastic empire biscuit. And which harled-wall avenues trudged were the most forlorn, while waiting for the end of the game.

It was New Year, and several decades before Scotland would be marketing itself as self-proclaimed world champs at Hogmanay. Methil was shut, life was shut, but the designation of 'holiday' – a semi-tragic misnomer – had compelled us to make this a full family outing. The football was all there was and if it was any consolation to my sisters, which I know it wouldn't have been, my team lost to the local favourites – ambushed in the dark.

I've never forgotten the unremitting gloominess of Bayview. The match was an afternoon kick-off and yet the sky was virtually starless and Bible black, a perspective not improved in the slightest by the floodlights. The illumination was patchy and one penalty box was so dingy it didn't look safe to venture there alone. The game was like kids way past their bedtime playing long bangers between garage doors under a single, sparking street lamp. And eventually the despairing cry rang out: 'For fuck's sake, will someone put another shilling in the bastardin' meter!'

But there's a far better story about East Fife and floodlights, and this one's truly tragic. It tells how an outstanding team were cast as 11 Icaruses, flew too close to the glow from the pylons and crashed to the ground, along with their hopes of becoming champions of Scotland.

In the winter of 1952–53, when English football declared, 'Let there be light,' the Bayview postie developed backache. Invite after invite arrived at the ground from clubs eager to have the fabulous Fifers handsel their floodlights. In the Methil boardroom, chests swelled, popping waistcoat buttons. In the case of the treasurer, maybe all of the top three.

But these floodlit friendlies were right bang in the critical, squeaky-bum part of the season. Between Saturdays in the league, sure-shot striker Charlie Fleming and his team-mates would trek long distances, sometimes to be the star attraction at two of these *son et lumière* spectaculars in rapid succession, with the first an epic 15 hours from the Kingdom by bus.

East Fife were an astonishing outfit. They'd re-emerged after the Second World War with the attitude 'Before we were so rudely inter-rupted …' and added the League Cup to the Scottish Cup hoisted just prior to football being suspended. The former would be won twice more in the next half-dozen seasons, a glistening spell which no Scottish club of such modest size has ever matched. But it could have been even more dazzling.

Methil's population was just 12,000, the equivalent of Ashby-de-la-Zouch or Hetton-le-Hole. Yet from these unlikely surroundings – with local history books noting the coal hoists and recording the arrival of underground public toilets as 'a big city feature for a small town' – East Fife were challenging Hibernian and Rangers, who in that era were dividing up the league between them.

Beginning at Gloucester City, the Fifers' attraction for English teams was irresistible. Though Fleming, nicknamed 'Cannonball', could do nothing to make the journey in a rudimentary charabanc, pre-motorways, happen any quicker, the team won 6–0. Twenty-four hours later they banged in seven against another non-league side, Worcester City. But come Saturday and the resumption of their title bid, East Fife would trip up at lowly Dundee.

It must have been exhausting, chasing the glow of 100,000 watts, for as well as all the travel and the games, the players were required at civic functions and sightseeing excursions, inspection of a tidal bore being typical, and never mind the bores in chains of office with which they would have to make small talk. Still, the invites to trip the light fantastic kept coming, the next from England's top flight, and Sunderland were left just as thumped, and just as grateful, for what the local paper on Wearside hailed as the 'artistry' of East Fife, a side with a 'sweet-moving attack' who administered a 'hiding' to the local favourites.

In 1952 the Harlem Globetrotters' embracing of comedy was complete with the recruitment of a stooge team to tour with them and be the butt of their basketball slapstick. A year later, East Fife must have had some in their English audiences wondering if they were still members of the Scottish League or had possibly run off to join a circus or become a Thomas Edison tribute act. They were moths to a flame, and not so much performing monkeys as owls or bats or other creatures of the night.

Yes, they were still fighting for the championship, but would drop more points to Partick Thistle and Celtic while honouring their commitments to Bristol City, Swindon Town, Notts County, Carlisle United and Newcastle United.

The floodlit friendlies jammed between league games almost required East Fife to be in two places at once. On any Big Top bill they would have been listed as illusionists/escapologists. But, like Harry Houdini manacled upside down in a water chamber, they were unable to pull off the final, miraculous showstopper and win the title. In their last three games in pursuit of it they claimed just a solitary point. Rangers were champs and East Fife, after so much promise, finished third.

So, were the club too polite to turn down all the invites? Or too greedy to pass up the appearance money? If, in those early days of fan accoutrement, you had the names of East Fife's lusty and loyal first XI stitched into your tammy or painted on your rattle – if you had revelled in this (black and) golden era and wished for the title to be the crowning glory – then there would have been heavy disappointment at how the season burned bright then fizzled out.

But it might just be possible to view 1952–53 in, well, a different light. What if the team were actually intrepid adventurers? What if, in the spirit of Mungo Park, they were engaged in important missionary work, teaching their English counterparts how the game, when bathed in shimmering lustre, could be even more exciting and even more beautiful? Britain was not long out of the Second World War. The Edinburgh International Festival, begun in 1947, and 1951's Festival of Britain were efforts to heal, renew, innovate – and emerge from darkness. Maybe East Fife did the same.

14

'Dan Brown vs the brown drink'

BOVRIL –
ACCEPT NO SUBSTITUTE

I've been here before. Running round noticeboards collecting 'To weds' and prize fish weights and newly elected office-bearers of the Rotary club. Vital info for a cub reporter on a small weekly newspaper, for sure, but I had no idea that this was Where It All Began.

By 'it' I mean life. Conspiracy theorists, bampots, impressionable saddos and Americans flock to the Midlothian village of Roslin because the chapel features in *The Da Vinci Code*. Dan Brown's novel is held up by its devotees as an alternative bible. A forest-devouring pulp monster, published long after I'd left the rag and so sparing me from having to write stories about the local connection, the book was a huge hit with gap-year youth and others with gaps between their ears. Unsurprisingly, the literati weren't impressed. 'Arse gravy of the worst kind,' snorted Stephen Fry.

Arse gravy? Maybe that's what you think of Bovril. But then you've probably never needed a hot drink so badly you'd have slurped down absolutely anything. You've almost certainly never been at the mercy, for instance, of the Cowdenbeath Kettle – not an industrial-sized urn but a standard domestic water warmer, requiring to be refilled constantly, while the survivors of a monsoon at the home of the Blue Brazil queued in puddle lakes at half-time behind the mirage of a catering van. You'd have craved whatever liquid could be squeezed out of cast-off jockstraps, then heated up, however slowly, on that godforsaken Saturday afternoon, oh yes, you would. And the house I'm standing outside – 29 Main Street, Roslin – is where Bovril began.

Why didn't I know this was the birthplace of John Lawson Johnston, Bovril's great alchemist? Why didn't I write 742 articles about this highly notable address, seven miles from Edinburgh, during my days on the *Dalkeith Advertiser*, nicknamed 'The Squeak'? The plaque above the door is a recent installation and I'd like to think it's a snap back at *The Da Vinci Code*, a reassertion of true history – meaningful and vital history.

When Napoleon demanded one million tons of beef to feed his soldiers during the Franco-Prussian War, he wasn't thinking about transportation or storage or the risk of alerting the enemy from so many clanking tins. Our man devised 'Johnston's Fluid Beef', taking his wizard wheeze into the trenches of the First World War and then on to the football terraces.

Come on, which would you prefer? Would you want to be quietly seething in a pretentious coffee shop – maybe some sort of hipster-heavy upcycled pop-up brunch caravan – and forced to watch the self-indulgent ceremony of 'limited-edition artisan roast' being prepared by a plonker with a backwoodsman beard, bare ankles showing, who calls himself a 'latte artist'? Or would you rather be served Bovril by a harassed but heroic middle-aged wifie, her bingo wings tensing for the first time in years with the stress, behind storm-battered Central Park, a place never, ever to be confused with Central Perk, where the beautiful people in *Friends* hung out for their caffeine fixes?

It has to be Bovril, and at the Cowden colosseum, even amid the thud of rain on corrugated metal, a sweet lament can always be heard: 'There was a coo, on yonder hill/There was a coo on yonder hill/It's no' there noo, it must have shifted/There was a coo on yonder hill.'

When you eventually get your drink you cradle that mass-produced polystyrene cup like you'd never let it go. Unless of course an opposition player does something to annoy you. Footballers most likely to have Bovril hurled at them? Here's a handful from the 1970s, but feel free to compile your own list: Willie McVie, the Scorsese hood in a Krazy Kutz bubble perm in the centre of the Motherwell defence; Alex MacDonald of Rangers, arch greetin'-faced proponent of the fly dunt; John MacDonald, Rangers' master of the penalty-box dive ('Ooh, I'm a starfish!'); roaring Aberdeen granny-kicker Davie Robb;* unsmiling Celtic brick outhouse Pat McCluskey. Of course you wouldn't mind these guys' complete lack of self-consciousness and imperviousness to abuse in your team.

Where would football be without Bovril? You can't have one without the other. You can't drink Bovril in July therefore summer football can never happen. It's Scotland's other, other national drink.

Bovril has its own classic American sitcom cachet, being namechecked in *Frasier*. And I also like to think of the modest commemoration of its origins in Roslin as a riposte to out-of-town stadia. Hearts and Hibernian could have ended up ground-sharing just along the road from the village which would have meant a grim traipse into the countryside for fans, past fields with cows in them and other unnerving sights – never mind that the Edinburgh rivals would have made strange bedfellows. Thankfully the move never happened and now the site is home to IKEA, a strange manufacturer of beds – they defy standard UK sizing – which is a much better use of the area's blasted-heath desolation.

Bovril probably doesn't hold the key to the meaning of life; unlike *The Da Vinci Code* it doesn't make that boast. But the brown drink vs Dan Brown? No contest.

---

* In his determination to reach a cross or win a tackle, Robb never actually assaulted his grandmother.

15

'We were warned not to get off with any footballers ... I ended up with Chick Young'

THE TENNENT'S CAN GIRLS

It was at the weekly newspaper that I took ownership of my second-ever porn stash. The first had been all the back copies of my father's *Amateur Photographer* magazine nicked from his study containing 'how to' hints for snapping the naked female form, though invariably and frustratingly the illustrations would be in silhouette. The second was the 'Car of the Week' drawer.

'Car of the Week' was a piece of advertorial about the best second-hand jalopy available through the paper's motoring pages and it was my job to phone up the relevant Swiss Toni* for a eulogy of smarm and quarter-truths, and then match the words to a generic shot from the office filing cabinet.

A lot of the cars had girls in bikinis draped across the bonnet. Was there ever a more uncomfortable pose than spreadeagled on the cold metal canopy of a beige-coloured saloon, assembled in Britain between go-slows and strikes? But girls in bikinis were everywhere in the mid-1970s. In Benny Hill sketches. Once national dress had been removed, in Miss World. On the sleeves of cheapo *Top of the Pops* LPs full of squawky cover versions of the Hit Parade. In the William Hickey gossip column in the *Daily Express*, the national

---

* Sleazy car salesman on *The Fast Show*

bulletin of dolly-bird activity and crumpet progress. And on cans of beer.

The Lager Lovelies were a bevy of bevvy-promoting models, and men who liked beer and women were smitten by them. For men who liked beer, women and football, the cans with so much luscious pouting on the sides were a one-stop shop.

Football fans already approved of cans wholeheartedly. As well as being drink receptacles they served as portable pissoirs for when the crowd was jam-packed and battling to the loos was too much trouble. They could transform into missiles, with or without the pee inside, when opposing supporters became annoying. But the cunning plan of utilising girls wearing not many clothes to advertise the product sent the cans hurtling into a whole other dimension.

Supporters had favourite girls who, they ardently believed, were their girls alone. No one could love their Lovely more, even if the bloke three steps further down the terracing was snuggling up to her too, whispering sweet nothings to a different incarnation of the tin-tube enchantress.

Fans would have sought out their special one on the shelves of their local Agnew's, rejecting the others like a cruel casting director waving away musical auditionees with a camp but decisive flutter of the hand. Caressing the cans in the stadium bowl, gripping tightly at moments of tension, they would have confided in their girl as the opposition team threatened to deny them victory, seeking reassurance in her unwavering lip-gloss pucker.

Originally, brewers Tennent's decorated the cans with stirring landscapes and stout buildings of note. Their lager was targeted at squaddies stationed abroad and this imagery was like a postcard from home. But there's a limit to the amount of pining that castles and cathedrals can induce. So Tennent's gave up on religion and went sex mad.

A woman started appearing in the foreground, the comely Ann. Typically she'd be placed in a waterfront setting and the caption would read: 'Waiting for the steamer at Loch Lomond'. Then more girls turned up. Then the steamers toppled over the far horizon. The home market demanded a look at these beauteous creatures and the lager instantly became a football favourite.

The relationship between drinker and drink plugger – how would we describe it? It might be tempting to think of the Lovelies or Can Girls as vaguely comparable to blow-up dolls, but really there was nothing weird about the association and not very much that was sleazy. Perhaps, if the fan bumped into his girl in the street in real, live 3-D form, he might quip: 'I hud ma hauns roond yez last night, hen.'

Unthreateningly, and in almost a debonair way, this definitely happened. The Lovelies weren't unattainable supermodels, completely out of the supporters' league. Maybe there wasn't an Isa or a Euphemia or a Senga or an Aggie – that would have been the actual dream team – but Linda and Lorna and Fiona and Heather simply seemed like the best-looking women who ever sold the fans a square sausage in a roll or the *Daily Record* or a pint in a pub.

At the photo shoots, to achieve the right look, the girls had to spend all afternoon in a wind tunnel. This reddened the cheeks and sometimes a bit more. When nipples appeared on the proofs they had to be airbrushed away. The cost of these chaste erasements is recorded for posterity at £3,000, presumably per pair. The image presented had to be like a copy of *Reveille* slipped inside *People's Friend*, rather than the other way round: sexy but homely, the goer next-door.

Maybe you or I couldn't have married a Lovely but Partick Thistle and Scotland goalie Alan Rough* did, and Posh and Becks were only able to effect a global celebrity perisher power-couple tyranny because Roughie and the one called Michelle had trailblazed the idea of a footballer and his WAG, only in their case with considerably more innocent charm.

The one called June remembers the world turning, the beginning

* See chapter 29

of political correctness and questions which went: 'What does it feel like to be exploited?' But she always defended the soft metal stunnas and their right to bring a little cheer to the rain-lashed stadium slopes. In this she was indomitable.

June was a beauty pageant regular. 'Miss Edinburgh, Miss Black Heart Rum and, er, Miss Scotland Wet T-Shirt,' she recalled. But it was Miss UK, shown on prime-time telly, which was 'the real cattle market' with a key segment of the adjudication concentrating on the contestants' arses.

'Compared to that, advertising beer was a lovely job,' June said. 'I was flown round the world to glamorous locations and paid well to have a great time.' The Lager Lovelies weren't sizeist – rather, bauchle-inclusive. 'I got to call myself a model despite being only 5ft 5ins and Can Girl was the ultimate,' June added. It brought her romance, too. 'One of my last jobs was with the Scotland World Cup squad. We were warned not to get off with any footballers ... I ended up with Chick Young.'

While June and Michelle snared fine specimens of Scottish manhood, the rest of the Lovelies were the bonnie, big-haired, football-tolerant, non-bossy, fun-loving dream girls of the terracing admass. For those years when alcohol at matches was permitted, the fans were like centurions celebrating their pre-eminence by swigging Posca, the vinegar-based wonder drink of the Roman Empire. More than that, cradling those sweethearts, not too tall and none too goddess-like, they were Antonys wooing their Cleopatras. And at the final whistle with the game won, you would have to conclude, in Shakespeare's words: 'In thy possession lies a lass unparalleled.'

16

'Quinty-whit?'

THE GREATEST SLOGAN TV'S
MAD MEN NEVER COINED

Words ping and zing in the football chitchatterama. Ping itself is one
– 'The ball was pinged over and Boydy* huckled it into the net, fell
on it, burst it with his big "say-aye-to-a-pie" belly.' The lexicon isn't
vast but seems sufficient for our needs. Still, you wonder if there
might be new, different and exciting words hiding somewhere which
could invigorate the debate.

Then you emerge from the darkness of the Clockwork Orange,
the Glasgow Underground. You are in the shadow of Ibrox. A sign,
glinting plasticky red on blue under the street lights, proclaims: 'The
Louden Tavern – the Quintessential Rangers Supporters Pub.'

Quintessential – you read it right. Not Quinton Young, nickname
Cutty, the straggle-haired occasional patrolman of the Govan left
wing in the mid-1970s. Not quince, a favourite jam of batty dowager
duchesses, and not quim, a word I learned from my father's porn
stash and the priapic odyssey *Walter – the Diary of a Victorian Gentle-
man*. It's okay for rock bands to call themselves Quintessence, as a
bunch of jazz 'n' raga-loving Notting Hill hippies did in the late 1960s.

---

* Kris Boyd, the former Rangers striker with a throwback poacher's eye for goal
and a throwback tubby girth.

It's okay for George Bernard Shaw to write an appreciation of Norwegian dramaturgy and title it *The Quintessence of Ibsenism*. And it's okay for old Billy Shakespeare to have Hamlet enquire: 'What is this quintessence of dust?' But can a fitba drinking den really be quintessential?

Imagine the conversation that might have taken place over the commissioning of this grandiloquent statement. 'Quinty-whit?' could have been the response of signwriters whose most daring work previously had been replacing the odd C with a K, e.g. for the Krazy Kutz hair salon and Kapital Kludgies.

For civic ostentatiousness and audacity, the Louden's claim to absolute perfection may be the Sagrada Familia of signage. As many letters as Antoni Gaudí's Barcelona cathedral has spires. Syllables jutting everywhere. But the banner is not incongruous at Rangers, one of the least shy and retiring clubs anywhere. These are fans who have appropriated the British flag, sing about being 'Simply the Best', refer to their stadium as the Big Hoose and chant: 'We are the peepul!'

Here's an example of how unshy Rangers are. It comes from Colin Stein, talking about the pre-match in his era, but the spirit holds true today: 'Everyone had their own wee dressing-room routine. Willie Henderson was the joker, Alex MacDonald was aye chirpy, Davie Provan would be throwing up, a fag or two for Willie Johnston in the bogs – and big Ronnie McKinnon would be slicking back his hair in the mirror, dead suave, and going: "Who are we playing the day? Do you think they'll turn up?"'

Unsurprisingly, the red, white and blue exterior of the Louden continues through the swing doors. Windowless, low-ceilinged and searingly lit, it's like being inside a Union Jack-swathed zorb. Like being trussed up in Ginger Spice's Girl Power minidress. Or wrapped in the flag carefully positioned behind the Tory cabinet minister telling us Brexit is going to make Britain great again. Or in the beach shorts the Ingurland skinhead has dropped so he can stick a firework up his bum.

The floor is blue, the chairs are red and the walls are white, though they're covered almost entirely in pennants, one for each of the 55 championships won by Rangers. Elsewhere: team shirts both sturdy and silk-like, old heroes and new ones, Brylcreem and bronzer, shaved-sides hairstyles (original and *Peaky Blinders*). The front of the long bar is criss-crossed like the shelf of Ibrox's Archibald Leitch-designed main stand. At one end, cartoon caricatures of Jock Wallace's Treble winners. At the other, Jim Baxter in stained-glass form eyes up the bottles of Bacardi.

There's music. A megamix of club anthems, some in the reggae style but most with a country-and-western twang and warble. Songs of Barcelona and Wolverhampton and 'dear old Ulster'. Songs about penny arcades, bluebells being blue and not surrendering. Sample lyrics: 'The badge on my breast ... the gun in my hand ... Our grandfathers fought ... staunch and true.'

This is transcendental Teddy Bearism. A sensory overload of Loyalism. A docked submersible of total Gerness. In short: quintessential.

This club have no need to feel intimidated by the word and it would hardly be a surprise if it had made its way into common Rangers parlance, or indeed common Rangers Parlane (after Derek, a team-mate of Cutty Young) ...

'Goal! Whit a goal! That was fuckin' quintessential Rangers, would you no' say, Billy? What we are aw aboot?'

'Well, Alec, it was a good goal, I'll gie you that, and an essential one, but quintessential? Naw. See, there was no George Young involved in the build-up, a big hoof and a follow-through on one of their guys, sending him over the enclosure wall. No Bachelor of Arts-with-Honours finessing from Slim Jim, and none from Gazza or Wee Prime Minister or Laudrup either. Greigy never swivelled that big arse of his yon serene way, like a faithful old Clyde steamer turning for home. And who scored the goal? Not Steiny or Super Ally or Coop right after a keepy-uppy masterclass. It was just a wee thow below quintessential, if you're askin' me.'

17

*'A double-headed sixpence wrapped
in a mystery inside a clootie dumpling'*

DUNDEE'S CONJOINED TWINS

If schoolboys in Lima and Karachi and, yes, even Hemel Hempstead know anything about Scottish football, it will be one of these three things and hopefully all of them: Arbroath 36 Bon Accord 0 is a world-record score; the league comprises Celtic, Rangers and some other clubs; two of these other clubs can be found at the same bus stop, are served by the same bin-lorry crew and not very long ago the sweet smell of jute carried on the breeze from the mills would reach them simultaneously.

There are just 200 yards between Dens Park, the home of Dundee, and Tannadice, where Dundee United do their thing. Two hundred – think about that. Two hundred is nothing. You could walk it in a few seconds, reciting the names of *The Broons* as you go. Redoubtable United backliner Jackie Copland, standing in the Tannadice penalty box, could enact his famous impersonation of a medieval trebuchet, hoofing a gigantic clearance over to Dens and Bobby Glennie would nonchalantly fire a cloud-burster right back at him. Usain Bolt could run the 200 yards faster than you could chew a mouthful of Dundonian 'peh' the medically advisable number of times before swallowing. Among the fans who are there every week, one place or the other, the 200 could be completed blindfolded, backwards, hopping.

But the proximity of Dundee to Dundee United is more than just a fancy-that fact. Personally, I think it's art. One of the seven wonders of Scotland alongside our great feats of engineering, the Forth Bridge and 1960s *Reporting Scotland* grande dame Mary Marquis's steepling bouffant, the lacquer holding fast like rivets. I was about to call the hugger-mugger dynamic of two football teams situationist art, though apparently the term isn't really concerned with your situation vis-à-vis a neighbour's situation and their nearness to each other. Shows what I know, but in a city of much municipal brutalism it's still art.

Various films come to mind here and in all of them the main characters are handcuffed together, always reluctantly. There's Robert De Niro's *Midnight Run*, the prisoner-and-escort buddy movie. There's *The Defiant Ones* about a black jailbird (Sidney Poitier) and a white one (Tony Curtis) on a breakout. There's Alfred Hitchcock's *The 39 Steps* with Robert Donat as a man of action entwined with a flibbertigibbet. The manacled protagonists are different people. They can't stand each other but survival depends on them getting along. And each time by the end grudging mutual respect turns to a kind of love.

Surely this is Dundee and Dundee United with, if you like, the Tay Bridge substituting for the Forth Bridge used by Hitchcock for his most dramatic set piece. These clubs profess to being sworn enemies but I seriously doubt this to be true. If they were really rivals, living cheek by jowl, wouldn't they have killed each other by now? If Rangers and Celtic were within slugging range like this there would be big, black, still-smouldering craters where the parks used to be.

During derbies the fans shout and scream in the direction of the other lot, and when Dundee had the chance in 2016 to relegate United, their supporters dressed as hangmen and undertakers and bore cardboard coffins. Vanquishment duly achieved, it was cheered right into the Dens rafters. But as a consequence of what became known as the Doon Derby, United were only departing the top division. Both tribes could continue to be publicly irritated by each other but secretly comforted by the fact that the other lot in the cosy, pretendy rivalry were plying their trade in the usual place.

There's something sweet about this, and something comical, too. Panto jokes too numerous to mention and too corny to repeat have been told about those 200 yards. Oh that William McGonagall had lived to see football establish itself on a hill above the silvery Tay.

So if Dundee and Dundee United were a comedy double act, which would it be? Maybe Mutt and Jeff whose get-rich-quick wheezes in a strip cartoon date from the first major trophy being carried into the city, Dundee's Scottish Cup of 1910, the same year United were voted into the league. Or Laurel and Hardy with one always lording it over the other. Or Steptoe and Son with one always threatening to leave the other but ending up precisely 200 yards away.

Seriously, I'm envious of this closeness and wish my team lived next door to the mob I feign hatred for. As a boy attending my first match in the city, at Dens, I made my father walk me round the inactive Tannadice before kick-off. Football tourists the world over must do the same on their pilgrimages. The dream date for those seeking the unique, never-to-be-repeated experience of a football fiesta spread across the two colosseums was 18 February 1968. Both hosted Scottish Cup ties on a thrilling two-peh afternoon beginning with 11 goals at Tannadice then moving on to Dens. What a Lowryesque scene there must have been with the approaches thronged with four sets of supporters, a swirling soup of bunnets and tammies.

Dundee and Dundee United are two peas in a pod, co-riders on a boneshaker tandem, a couple of swells, a double-headed sixpence wrapped in a mystery inside a clootie dumpling, the last pair of chocolates left in the box. The coffee cream and the lime barrel, however, always look forlorn; these two positively glisten in the aerial photographs, a juxtaposition which makes you smile every time. Yes, they are couthie like Fran and Anna and the Alexander Brothers, but they also resemble those living sculptures, Gilbert and George, for I repeat: this is art. In 2018 the V&A opened in Dundee amid great hullabaloo, but the museum instantly had to take its place behind the city's most lustrous cultural gem, the T&D (Tannadice and Dens).

One club cannot taunt the other about their fans living in slums or of their stadium being a piggery or everyone being on heroin because all of this would apply to them, too. In 2017, Dundee – playing the part of the aspirational Harold Steptoe who convinces himself he's outgrown his parochial, repetitive existence – donned its velvet jacket and attempted to leave again. Plans were unveiled for a new ground in a country park to the west of the city. In the future, Dundee propose, the distance between the clubs should be three miles – too far to walk to borrow a cup of sugar or a turnstile key, or to first-foot on New Year's Day.

But, really, will the separation ever happen? Two-berth buggies trundle and squeak in a city which has a claim to being the teenage pregnancy capital of Europe, but Dundee and Dundee United are the world's oldest-surviving conjoined twins. If the wrecking ball was to scud into the side of one stadium, the other would cry out in pain. (Then it would write a letter to 'The Doc' at the *Sunday Post* joining all the lumbago and haemorrhoid sufferers in seeking a remedy.)

There is no escape for the Tayside twosome, unless it's in a double coffin. When it's dark and late and deserted on Sandeman Street and no one is around, do they sidle over to each other and snuggle up to keep out the cold? Well, how do you know that they don't?

18

'I grabbed the pigeon and threw it at the clown'

JOHN LAMBIE, CHARACTER

I was surveying the home of a true football man, spotting the playing-days mementos and the cup given to him for being a 'manager extraordinaire'. I was noticing the family photos, also the snap of him with Chic Charnley, an incorrigible rascal he signed four times and who, by way of thanks, phoned the old boss every week just to check he was doing okay. But, for the life of me, I couldn't find any erotic art.

Was there a nude I simply wasn't seeing, a languorously reclining figure in the style of Modigliani, with the muse having been a Partick Thistle tea lady taking the load off her bunions after the half-time rush? Or a depiction in the altogether of a Hamilton Accies cleaner, Klimt-style? Nope. There were no fabulously spherical Rubenesque creatures letting it all hang out in John Lambie's Bathgate maisonette, no Botticelli-like nymphs.

Haltingly, I read out the last line of Lambie's Wikipedia entry, how post-football, post-hairy-arsed changing rooms, painting the human form in the scud was his thing. 'Whit?' he snapped from his favourite armchair, slippers twitching. 'Nah, that's no' me. Some bugger's at the wind-up.'

Some bugger was. And it was totally unnecessary. Lambie's story had no need of such embellishment. It's often said the game these days lacks characters. That was him, all right. A one-stop character shop. The character's character. A character to the max, to the nth degree, topped off with character sauce. Some might have gasped, 'You're killing us; it's character overload!', but not me.

In a career of mischief and mayhem – and miraculous victories – Wiki's purple prose could have come from just about any board-room, any dressing room. Normally I might have been disappointed such a racy revelation had been rubbished but this was Lambie, who'd enlivened the party with his ranting, White owl cigars and savage humour, and the yarns were still good. They could plunge you so deep inside a West Lothian netherworld of dog tracks and dodgy characters that you might have forgotten to ask him to repeat, one more time for the people, the Dead Pigeon Sketch.

This was when a Partick player irritated the doo-fancying Lambie to the extent the manager felt compelled to wallop him with a pigeon which had expired, ceased to be, was bereft of life – or very nearly. 'Declan Roche just wouldn't shut up. I had a bird which I was about to let go at our training field but got so pissed off I took it out of the basket and threw it at the clown.'

Now, when Lambie died in 2018, obituaries stated that a different player, Paul Kinnaird, was the victim, which begs the question: did he do this twice? You wouldn't have put it past him.

Son of a miner, grandson of a town provost, nobody's fool. Suffi-ciently open-minded as a manager, and as a Church of Scotland worshipper, to embrace the teachings of American televangelist Joyce Meyer. 'I got hooked on one of her self-help books and, honestly, turned myself. All negative thoughts went right oot the windae.'

All of which whisked us, effortlessly, to a windae in Aviemore, Thistle's base for a tour of the Highlands: 'The night before the first game I got told some of my players were sneaking lassies into their rooms. I headed straight for the likeliest offenders, my two strikers, who took an awful long time answering their door. Nae girls, but I'm sure my hunch was right. "Lads, here's what I want you to do tomorrow," I said. "When we're attacking, one of you makes a near-post run and the other checks out and comes in at the back stick." They were wondering why I was dishing out tactics at gone ten o'clock at night. Eventually there was a bang on the windae and some wailing. Four lassies had been hiding on the balcony wearing just their knickers. That was a costly tour for seven of the team: £500 fines each, including Colin McGlashan, a lovely lad who never really caused me any trouble, and moaned: "But I never even got a kiss!"'

If it was any consolation to McGlashan, he would be the fall guy for peak Lambie, the apogee of the man's apoplectic wit. Unsnogged and suddenly unconscious, the player had been knocked out during a hectic game at Thistle's Firhill. The physio relayed an urgent message back to the dugout: 'It's concussion, gaffer. He's got no bloody idea who he is.' Lambie's response propelled him into the echelons of the most quotable, just behind Winston Churchill, Martin Luther King and Davina McCall: 'Slap that fuckin' wet sponge on his face and tell him he's fuckin' Pelé.'

Lambie when we met was primed and ready with the funny yarns. How, to whip up publicity for Hamilton Accies, he pretended a miserable ten-game losing streak was costing him nookie at home only for his wife in her embarrassment to institute a real sex ban.

How, also at Hamilton, he'd only show potential foreign signings round the modest town and even more modest ground under the cloak of darkness. When recruiting, he sought out 'heid-bangers' because they were winners. The biggest of them was Chic Charnley, the type who could score goals from halfway and, when confronted by a Samurai sword, pick up a parking cone and win the duel. 'I don't know what that incident was all about but I got the hell out of the way,' laughed Lambie. 'The guys who turned up asking for Chic were obviously severely dischuffed with him. He could have been the greatest but he knew all the rogues of the day. Don't get me wrong, I knew a few myself.'

But, much as he perpetuated the idea of football being a long-running slapstick comedy with Netflix-style content warnings –

'Nudity, smoking, language, threat, gore, injury to humans, injury to animals, injury to humans caused by animals used as close-combat weapons' – this can detract from his achievements, not least master-minding the 1987 Scottish Cup victory at Ibrox when Accies stunned the millionaires of Graeme Souness's Rangers.

Preparation was a trip to Blackpool, which just happened to coincide with Britain's biggest pigeon show. 'I think in my life I've understood pigeons better than I have footballers – and actually greyhounds better than the doos,' he admitted. Kevin McKee, Lambie's most nervous player, was up against Rangers' most outrageously skilful in Davie Cooper, but some of Joyce Meyer's positivity sorted out the imbalance and the result so shocked Souness that, while magnanimous in defeat when shaking hands with Lambie, he would soon be putting his foot through a TV set. Even the best can be heid-bangers sometimes.

As for the very best, Pep Guardiola is obviously a fantastic coach. An intense perfectionist who magicks dazzling stratagems. But could he do with lightening up? Overthinking one game too many might cause him to suffer a blackout. If that were to happen, then maybe this message could be conveyed to the self-combustible genius: 'You're John Lambie, you really are ...'

19

*'Like a Mellotron on top of a piano
on top of a Hammond organ on top
of a double-necked guitar'*

THE EDINBURGH DERBY
BEATS HITLER

In the underground nerve centre where the Second World War is being choreographed, anxious generals scrutinise the giant table map, hands clasped tightly behind their backs, while demure WAAFs stay calm to fulfil the task you will crave as a kid watching old battle movies decades later and still fancy even now – shoving model planes around with long sticks.

'Bit of a weather issue on New Year's Day, sir.'

'Go on …'

'The forecast is for fog on the Forth, sir.'

'So the public know the drill. Carry on as normal. Better still: like spring has sprung four months early. The young men of Edinburgh's fancy should lightly turn to thoughts of love. Not lightly – heavily. Let's have a mass outbreak of romantic cavorting on the streets. No one should be cowering indoors, inviting Jerry to launch a few Messerschmitts. The dour Calvinist air must be thick with longing. What say you, Miriam?'

'Yes, sir, very good, sir. But if it's thick with fog the traditional Hibernian vs Heart of Midlothian football match will have to be postponed. Learning this from cracking into the BBC Radio Home Service, Jerry will be alerted to perfect weather conditions for an attack.'

'Then the game must be played, Miriam. And, what's more, commentated upon.'

On 1 January 1940 at Easter Road it was a pea-souper all right. If the stadium had been a giant pot of real broth then even the most hard-line granny would have thinned it down. If the stadium had been a theatre for Gothic melodrama then the audience would have wailed: 'Normally we get the tops of graveyard headstones peeking out of the spooky mist at least, maybe a rook in a shrivelled tree. We can't see anything!'

The crowd couldn't see the players, the players couldn't see the ball. It must have been hugely surreal and frustrating for the teams, the officials and the 12,000 fans who'd felt their way along tenement walls to reach the ground. But the radio audience, at home and among the forces on foreign fields, were gripped by the most exciting match ever played. The man at the microphone, Bob Kingsley, made sure of that.

Told he had to voice the game as if it was a bright, clear day, his first idea was to station runners the length of the pitch who would pass descriptions of play in a relay back to the commentary box. But this quickly broke down, possibly because the intelligence was too slow in reaching Kingsley or maybe one of the runners disappeared into the murk and never returned. Then again the words could have become mangled, much like how the First World War's 'Send reinforcements we're going to advance' was turned into 'Send three and fourpence we're going to a dance'.

What now? This war could come Edinburgh's way if Kingsley didn't find some football to talk about. So he made it up. He invented an entire match. A good decade before the advent of free jazz, he turned his mic into an alto sax and went off on one. A good 30 years before the emergence of prog rock, his performance was like a Mellotron on top of a piano on top of a Hammond organ on top of a double-necked guitar – completely over the top.

Kingsley was perfect for this. More than just a commentary was needed and he was more than just a commentator. First he'd been an actor, learning the craft at the splendidly named Percival Steed's Drama School in his native Glasgow. He'd stood on stage at the city's tough variety theatres and got out alive. When, in 1924, he became the full-time announcer of the BBC's new Glasgow station, his audition involved disentangling the gnarly pronunciations in *A Swedish Composer's Night*. The challenge could just as easily have been: 'Invent a game of football.'

At the Beeb's Dundee outpost, storytelling skills were finessed on *Children's Hour* where he was 'Uncle Bob'. For the grown-up audience he'd taken charge of large-scale operatic dramas. He was just as adept at small-scale, though, juggling many voices and dialects. A critic raved: 'An American, a Scotchman, a widow, a small girl – it was hard to believe there weren't four people in the room.'

Everything he did seemed to be preparation for his finest hour and a half in the gloaming of Easter Road. He'd moved to sport and brought pizzazz to commentating. He'd switched to journalism, becoming the *Sunday Mail*'s star football writer – with the pen name Rex – and introducing humour to the back pages, having reasoned: 'The public were being stuffed with facts – facts which everyone in the crowd could see for himself. Facts can be dull.'

Here was a game bereft of facts although sadly no recordings survive of Kingsley's narration so we will have to imagine what he imagined. But guess what? The match might have been even more thrilling than his descriptions of delirious dribbles, cannonball shooting, thundering tackles etc. The final score – maybe just a rough guess – was Hibs 5 Hearts 6.

The crowd were only informed this brilliant, heroic farce had ended ten minutes after the players had left the pitch. Twenty-two had strode into the swirling mist but only 21 came back. In the Hearts dressing room there was some anxiety: where was Johnny Donaldson? A search party was mustered and the winger was eventually found, doggedly patrolling his beat on the left flank and vainly hollering for a pass from team-mates who were already in the communal bath.

Never was so much owed by so many to these 22. But everyone was indomitable that day, including the bemused fans and of course Kingsley, who'd remarked of the war: 'Doesn't it get you down? Just when the youngsters in football are busy earning their spurs, this German clown upsets everything.' Well, Adolf Hitler didn't drop any bombs on Edinburgh that day. The message to him from Scottish football was: 'Fog off.'

20

*'What country, no matter how desperate,
sticks a goalie outfield during a World Cup?'*

BOBBY CLARK
LEAVES HIS LINE

Down in Argentina in 1978 there was no water in the swimming pool and no nets on the tennis courts. Some of the mattresses on the beds had no springs, some of the rooms no windows, and the menu offered tough horse steak relentlessly. Holed up at the Sierras Hotel, Alta Gracia, goalkeeper Bobby Clark and the Scotland team had to make their own fun with plenty of time to ponder the ongoing World Cup nightmare.*

How to stop going insane? Postcards. They became Clark's great project and his room-mate Stuart Kennedy witnessed the obsession first-hand: 'Bobby fired them off to everyone he'd ever met and more than one per person. No way could I keep up with him.'

The pair would sit by the bone-dry crater, Clark a fastidious fellow with his DAKS blazer draped carefully on the back of a spare chair and a dictionary close at hand. 'He was never without it, kept it in the pocket of the DAKS,' continued Kennedy. '"Stuart, I strongly advise you to invest in one of these," he would say to me. Bobby is

---

* Propelled to Argentina by a Graf Zeppelin full of hot air, hullabaloo and hype, Scotland's big balloon burst after just one game when they were ambushed by Peru and lost winger Willie Johnston to a drugs ban.

very precise and methodical, always in control. When an old pal who'd emigrated to Australia popped into his head during these post-card sessions he was able to remember the full address. He was like Mr Memory in a variety show: "It's … it's Boomerang … no, wait, it's coming … Billabong Avenue! … And the number: one-four-eight … five!" That was a moment of triumph on the trip and bloody hell we didn't have many of those.'

But when you make postcards your life's work, even your tempo-rary life's work, then eventually you will lose control and go mad. Especially when the choice of image never varies from 1) Equestrian statues of Buenos Aires, 2) River Plate waterscapes, 3) The World Cup's cartoon gaucho mascot and 4) Stadia shot from the air. 'Always the same four themes,' confirmed Kennedy. 'Every other day we'd traipse down to the local shop to see if Pepe, the proprietor, had got in some different stock but he never had. And the moment I thought Bobby had properly lost it was after a bounce match at training. This was in the lead-up to the Holland game, the do-or-die one. [Manager] Ally MacLeod had told us that every single place in the team was up for grabs. Gordon McQueen was injured so the bouncer Bobby had filled in for him in defence. No way was that a legitimate audition, although he seemed to think it had been a great success.

"'Well," he said, "I reckon that's me straight into the side. Meet your new Scotland centre-half."

"'I don't think so, Clarky," I said. "What country, no matter how desperate, sticks a goalie outfield during a World Cup?"

"'But Ally told us that the players who perform best will be selected and did I not just dominate Joe Harper, first minute till last? No, Stuart, the manager has to remain true to his word otherwise he will lose my respect."

'So I had to tell him: "Clarky, you're a Corinthian, a Queen's Park amateur who went to university. You're Wilson of the *Wizard* who sleeps in a bath of ice and has a pulse rate of one and a fine square jaw and you look top-hole in your DAKS with wee Joey tucked in the breast pocket. But come on, man – you're a bloody keeper!"'

He was, and a good one, but maybe Clark, this precision guy, had suddenly developed an allergic reaction to the exactness of his box and a role defined and restricted by those regulation 18 yards. *The Goalkeeper's Fear of the Penalty* had been an art-house movie. Here was the sequel: The Fitba Custodian's Existential Crisis Re Typecasting. Kennedy might also have wondered if – blimey – his friend was about to grow his sensible hair long and throw away his dictionary.

In fact, Clark was merely remembering when he'd played outfield for real. He actually did this. It's always a tingly, tantalising moment when a goalie abandons his area to belt up the other end for an injury-time corner-kick and everyone holds their breath. Well, in 1969–70 Clarky made this moment last an entire 90 minutes.

When I spoke to him about it, Manuel Neuer, Germany's famed sweeper-keeper, had just claimed third place in the Ballon d'Or with West Ham United's Spanish No. 1 Adrian scoring the winning penalty in an FA Cup shoot-out. Clark topped their daring even if he didn't quite stroll through the emergency stint at stopper in his DAKS.

'Looking back, it does seem extraordinary,' he said, 'but I lost my place in the Aberdeen first team after letting in six goals against Hibs and then our defenders started getting injured. It was our grand old trainer Teddy Scott who nominated me for centre-half. Initially this was in the reserves and I made my debut against Clyde at Shawfield, being careful to remember to head the ball and not catch it. Soon I was quite enjoying my new life, safe in the knowledge there were only three men and a dog who were ever watching me.

'But then Martin Buchan got hurt in a car accident, leaving a gaping hole in the big team's defence. Suddenly I was on the bench at Ibrox. Suddenly I was out there in front of 40,000, far from my box, jousting with Colin Stein and his incredibly sharp elbows.' When Clark found himself in the centre circle of a proper big game he must have felt like he was completely naked, save for the clown's nose. 'After that came my first start as Aberdeen's No. 5 at St Johnstone and it didn't take me long to get a wee bit carried away. Instead of quickly passing the ball to someone who knew what to do with it, I was taking a couple of touches, then three, then four …'

It seems that Clark gave careful thought to the risks involved in daunering from his line and, with that calm, analytical mind, decided: 'Woo-hoo!' The experiment had been the most tremendous fun, an out-of-body and out-of-box experience, like the dependable drummer emerging from the dark of the rock stage and swinging the singer's mic at the swooning girls in the front row.

But it was never going to become permanent. Pittodrie manager Eddie Turnbull, the old-school disciplinarian, was far from vague and indecisive in his closing verdict: 'Hey you! You're a fuckin' goalie. That's it.'

And that was indeed it. Clark would go on to win a clean sweep of domestic honours and legendary status by staying right between the sticks. And he probably never thought any more about playing outfield until Argentina, a place where even clever men in smart blazers could end up going a little bit round the bend.

21

'Eight Flumps, twelve Bubblies, four Fruit Salads, six Flying Saucers'

ALEX MILLER, ICE-CREAM MAN

Wonderful images from Scottish popular culture present themselves when Alex Miller reveals his other job: the one he did right after finishing his shift as a Rangers player.

There's Miller being arithmetically challenged by two housing scheme urchins. One of them asks: 'How much for eight Flumps, twelve Bubblies, four Fruit Salads, six Flying Saucers, one packet of prawn cocktail crisps, a Shrimp and a bottle of ginger?' Sensing this is a rhetorical question, that the lad could be a student of Keynesian economics in a Tacchini trackie, Miller uses all of his fingers to tot up the price, only to be told: 'Just a penny chew then, Mister.'

Then there's Miller caught in the middle of a deadly turf war, a vicious battle over prime territory, everyone fighting dirty and ignoring historical rights and prepared to kill to get what they want. Miller, who might have been a contract tackler at Ibrox learning his chop kicks from a fuzzy pirate Bruce Lee VHS which played out of sync, is reluctant to get involved in this struggle. But he must offer some resistance and so arms himself with chocolate sauce squirters.

We're talking ice-cream vans, and while you may be familiar with these scenes from a TV commercial for a recruitment company and the Bill Forsyth comedy *Comfort and Joy*, Miller's stint as a mobile gelato vendor was no joke. He had a van. With a prominent cone at the prow like a unicorn's horn. And chimes. The only area of doubt concerns headgear: did this 1970s Ibrox tough guy sport a dinky soda jerk hat straight out of a Norman Rockwell painting?

Miller was nearing the end of his career clattering into Celtic players, and wondering what he might do with the rest of his life. He fancied coaching but then so did a lot of soon-to-be ex-pros and maybe he wouldn't get the opportunity. When he wasn't clattering he could be almost invisible: the 12th man, the utility man, the player's player, the guy doing the unglamorous work and being damned with faint praise for it.

The day I met Miller, he wasn't getting much praise of any sort from his wife Ann. He was recalling a fine goal he scored to win an Old Firm derby but also how he checked himself during his celebration – 'A wee jump, then control, composure' – when she interjected: 'That was you, all right – always did things by the book.' Miller, with pride but also pique, said: 'I was a staff sergeant in the BBs.' Mrs M continued the joshing: 'You'd never race through a red light.' Our man: 'Whereas you would!'

But, post-career, Miller didn't lack resourcefulness. Or initiative. Maybe he could go into business for himself, but as what? Pubs didn't sound like his thing. His non-drinking astonished Ibrox team-mates almost as much as his non-swearing. The van became available through a friend of his brother. He could learn how to keep books and understand VAT while sprinkling hundreds and thousands on toerags' shivery treats.

The beat was Clydebank. Miller would send Ann up to the local high school at lunchtime while he was training, then he'd take over for the evening run in the Goldenhill and Hardgate housing estates. And right after games you'd find him putting in a couple of hours. 'Of course I used to get some funny looks,' he said. 'Folk would be like: "Hang on, didn't I see you trip over the ball at Ibrox today?"'

In swapping sliding tackles for sliders, Miller did not expand the van's merry-melodies playlist to include a plinky-plink version of

'The Sash'. No point in halving your potential market before you've begun.

When Scotland's housing schemes were plonked on to outlying ground, they weren't over-endowed with amenities so ice-cream vans became general stores on wheels. The mob violence of Glasgow's Ice Cream Wars erupted over the most profitable patches after vans started offering drugs and stolen goods under the counter – did the conflict raspberry ripple in Miller's direction? 'Once another van did try to come on to my run,' he said. 'I got it stopped but I'd better not tell you how …'

The stint at the side window was short and sweet. Miller was never able to experiment and innovate like the *Comfort and Joy* brigade who pioneered ice-cream fritters – Frosty Hots. But it says something about him that he trundled and jingled down this unusual path; few footballers are brave enough to risk such potential ridicule.

He got to coach eventually. Indeed he manned dugouts from Paisley to Siberia, where little refrigeration is required, and won a cup for Hibernian when it seemed like the club, near-bankrupt, was about to melt away for ever.

In spite of that success, Miller continued to be underrated in the dugout until he dramatically turned up at Liverpool and, even more dramatically, helped them win the Champions League as Rafa Benitez's No. 2.

The incredible comeback from three–nil down against A.C. Milan in 2005 was more than Miller's apotheosis: it was the 99 flake atop the prize exhibit in the Mr Whippy Sculptor of the Year Contest (West of Scotland Region). At a key moment in Istanbul, he was glimpsed whispering in Benitez's ear, possibly his suggestion for a tactical rejig, and who's to say the new formation wasn't delineated in special code?

'Three Cola Bottles, two Blackjacks, a Chocolate Skull and two Sherbet Dabs …'

22

'Cod-classical codswallop in codpieces'

RICK WAKEMAN'S
WONDEROUS STORY

Music-wise, is there a greater gulf than the one between progressive rock's grandest folly and the novelty hit about running in the scud in public places?

Surely nothing connects *Tales from Topographic Oceans* to 'The Streak', even though they were released just weeks apart. There can be no common ground for Yes, who were taking themselves very seriously, and Ray Stevens, who was taking himself very frivolously. The latter's comedy 45 was a piece of fluff. *Tales* was epoch-making, but tragically not in the way Yes wanted it to be. Indulgence upon bombast upon rampant pretentiousness, the album pretty much did for prog. If proggers really did live in splendiferous castles with cloud-busting spires, then the gatekeepers were fast asleep when an unholy rabble of punk rockers charged across the drawbridges.

Never the twain shall meet? Oh yes, they will. Underestimate Scottish football at your peril. It has the power – the bonkers allure – to bring together disparate souls and be a safe house for the unlikeliest of allies.

Two such are Rick Wakeman and Terry Christie. The former, keyboardist in Yes, was most often glimpsed in a long golden gown matching his long golden girlie tresses. Contrastingly, the latter was hardly ever seen without his duffle coat, befitting a head teacher, but he was also the manager of little Meadowbank Thistle and, phantasmagorically, would welcome Wakeman into the fold as one of the hardy few in the windblown stand, not just as a supporter but the regular radio reporter.

Improbable and incredible as this may seem, Christie can match it with his 'Streak' story, his 'How I met my wife' story. Which do you want to hear first? Let's start with Wakeman ...

With *Tales*, Yes thought they were taking rock to the top of the pointiest steeple on a dreamscape gatefold sleeve painted by prog's artist-in-residence, Roger Dean. In fact, they were driving it to the bottom of a Dean lake. This was certainly where the *New Musical Express* wanted prog to be. 'The *Titanic* sails at dawn,' raged a famous headline, and the 'inkie', in thrall to the nascent punk clatter, was all for press-ganging every combo in capes flaunting tricky time changes and a giant gong – every exponent of cod-classical codswallop in codpieces – straight on to the doomed liner.

Wakeman, though, jumped ship. He was confused as anyone by the lyrics 'Craving penetrations offer links' and 'Release forward tallest rainbow'. And in a roundabout way – and 'Roundabout' was one of Yes's earlier, shorter, catchier numbers – this is how he washed up at Meadowbank.

It shouldn't have happened. Size was everything for bands like Yes. Length of songs, length of masturbatory soloing within songs, length of articulated lorries for the lugging of equipment. Number of Moogs and Mellotrons (R. Wakeman: 36). He should have become a celebrity cheerleader for one of the big dogs, Manchester United or Real Madrid, and not a scrawny stray like the other Thistle. Funny old game, prog rock.

Thus, Wakeman swapped a complicated life – a blizzard of musical notes, an imperfect storm of crashing arpeggios – for the simple one of a small football club, just seven years old, a knot of nutty fans and extremely modest dreams. He exchanged 'Wonderous Stories' for blunderous bulletins of sturdy-hurdy endeavour. And he traded fairy-tale donjons for municipal brutalism and one of the unloveliest buildings in the city of Robert Adam's magisterial crescents.

How did it happen? In 1981 Wakeman was rock-raconteuring on Edinburgh-based Radio Forth – and maybe at that precise moment he was explaining how drum solos in prog were so long he could order a curry from the stage and wolf it down before the sticksman had ceased his terrible thrashing – when suddenly his pregnant wife had to be whisked off to hospital. Osama bin Laden: when we met, this was what he called Nina Carter, the ex-Page 3 girl and third Mrs Wakers – at least until he remembered the crippling divorce bill. But the emergency was real.

'There were huge complications, a very good chance Nina could lose the baby, so she couldn't be moved,' he said. For three months, Wakeman stayed at Aberlady House in East Lothian, the grand abode of Forth supremo Richard Findlay. Between visits to Carter's bedside as her condition stabilised, there was opportunity for malarkey. 'Hibs trained on the beach near Richard's pile and I fell in with great characters like Alan Rough.'

Jim White, when Sky Sports' Partridge-esque presenter was at Scottish Television, got to hear about the friendship between one fellow who was highly dexterous and another who was a Scotland goalie and thought it would make a humorous 'And finally ...' item for the teatime news. 'We got pretty pissed and Jim still had to go on air,' added Wakeman. 'The STV anchorwoman introduced him: "Tell us what happened when you met the rock star, Jim ..." He was sniggering like a naughty schoolboy. "Er, we all ended up in the pub and shtayed there for quite shum time."'

After that, Wakeman possibly thought: football reporting, it's not exactly the stuff of Woodward and Bernstein, is it? So when Findlay suggested that to earn his keep the lodger might supply critiques of Meadowbank's games for Forth's listeners, he was up for it.

Meadowbank, as it happens, were quite punk. Switching analogies from dogs to children, they assumed the role of the spotty, awkward, surprise third child of the Edinburgh football scene. In the Soviet-style athletics arena which served as their home, the changing-room lockers required 10p pieces, which irritated Alex Ferguson, down with his Aberdeen team for a friendly. Sharing the space with shot-putters and javelin-throwers was hazardous. One bust-up ended with Christie being knocked to the ground, possibly grateful to have only been punched.

He was well used to the slings and arrows. His school was in one of the capital's most blighted corners with zero amenities, homes riddled with dampness, also heroin. One window-smashing spree left 90 of them gaping and when a golf ball flew into Christie's study while interviewing a candidate for a teaching post, the beak was unimpressed by this hopeful diving for cover and ruled him far too timid for the job.

In the spirit of punk's absolute democracy, Italian waiters claiming to be decent with a ball at their feet would be invited to train with Meadowbank. Fergie dubbed the team 'anti-football', but they would embarrass the big boys in cups. Wakeman, from a world of gargantuanism, loved all of this. Christie, loving neither punk nor prog, wouldn't have expected a daft ditty with the refrain 'Boogity, boogity' to assume deep and lasting personal significance, but this was 'The Streak'.

At his previous school he was supervising one of the Friday night discos when, just after the ode to spontaneous disrobing had been spun, a boy rushed up to him in a state of high anxiety. 'Sir, sir!' the lad blurted out. 'You'd better get along to the girls' cloakroom quick: there's a lassie saying she's going to streak and she's daft enough to do it.'

This was Susan. The bashful Christie was able to persuade the already half-undressed 16-year-old that a Lady Godiva impression really wasn't the best idea. Flash forward ten years to Edinburgh's Americana nightspot: 'I was 43 and divorced from Margaret, a lovely woman who couldn't cope with my football obsession anymore. One of my players, Mickey Lawson, had dragged me there because I'd been living like a monk. I must have cut a pretty gloomy figure and was about to shoot the crow when Mickey suggested we dance with these two women. The blonde one turned round, took one look at me and went: "Aagh!" She wouldn't stop screaming. It was Susan, and I'm afraid I couldn't produce a better chat-up line than: "Sorry, I didn't recognise you with your clothes on." That was 1985 and we've been together ever since.'

Sadly, no recordings remain of Wakers at the mic for Meadowbank, breathlessly describing 0–0 draws with Alloa Athletic, or even 5–5 draws, but the club which grew out of an engineering factory side and subsisted in the shadows of Hibs and Hearts remember a jolly fellow who liked a beer or eight and would send himself up but never his all-new favourite football team.

I'd like to think his sporting gesture was not just a thank-you to Edinburgh but an apology for the bleak midwinter of 1973 when Yes brought their *Tales* tour to the capital. On a bitterly cold morning at the old Empire Theatre, me and some pals from the third form queued for five hours for tickets, then on the evening of the show waited for two bingo sessions to empty for the music to start, just before midnight. I liked prog, and especially liked that it might make me appear deep, clever and fanciable to the trainer-bra temptresses back at school, so would flaunt the sleeves back and forth across the quad as – cue Norman Mailer – advertisements for myself. But I didn't know *Tales* – none of us did as the record hadn't been released – and yet Wakeman & Co. performed it in its entirety, one infernal 'suite' after the other. It was a tough listen; it was a trigonometry exam. 'That was brilliant!' we chorused, setting off on the walk home through slush-filled streets, the last bus having long gone. Inside, though, we were screaming.

To top it off, Wakeman knocked me back for an autograph. This was during the soundcheck and, dismayingly, he was already dressed in his shimmering cloak, which spoiled the grand entrance later. 'Can't do it, mate,' he said, 'otherwise they'll all want one. And just look at how many keyboards I've got to tune ...'

Unfortunately, he didn't wear his golden gown to the Golden Gates, the pub across from Meadowbank Stadium where the Thistle fans gathered to toast their smallness and spikiness. Wakeman remembered his first visit: 'The initiation ceremony was a raffle in which I seemed to be the only contributor. The seller was this charming fellow who merely grunted. After I'd seen off something like the 18th roll of tickets I asked him: "When's the draw, by the way?" The barman said: "There's no prizes, he just likes taking money off prats like you."'

Yes were the band who constructed such an elaborate pod for their drummer that, if oxygen pumps and pickaxes hadn't been handy, it might have swallowed the poor sap whole – but while Wakeman bunked off from prog, he didn't completely renounce it. He dreamed up his own excess – the legend of King Arthur, performed on ice – and eventually drifted back to Yes, possibly to help pay the divorce costs.

But he really loved Meadowbank Thistle, that odd career interregnum and its happy ending. He said: 'Eventually, my daughter Jemma arrived safe and well. Terry the manager came to the hospital and gave her a teddy in the club colours, yellow and black. She's a musician herself now and she still has it.'

Today, the bear's shirt is out of date, as is the name. Meadowbank became Livingston when the club relocated to the new town with its 542 roundabouts. Then the Golden Gates disappeared, followed by the stadium. But the most famous fan still roots for them. Performing at the Edinburgh Festival the summer we spoke, Wakers sang the praises of a city dear to him, although he was adamant it was missing something special: 'For my team to move back there and be called Meadowbank Thistle again.'

23

*'I suppose they were expecting
me to drop down dead'*

WHOLEHEARTED
ASA HARTFORD

Five years before, we had held our breath. The heart? Even with little proper understanding of physiology and only 'Made in Hong Kong' plastic stethoscopes at our disposal, we knew that in the league table of vital organs it was right up there. How ever would Christiaan Barnard's transplant work, taking from one human and placing in another? So we were hooked on the news updates and maybe these were more gripping than even the Apollo mission dispatches because of being more relatable. Hardly any of us had rockets but we all had hearts.

Asa Hartford had a hole in his, discovered as he was about to move from West Bromwich Albion to Leeds United in 1971. The world, not just football, was shocked.

Career over? Worse than that? ...

'I signed for Leeds on the Wednesday and the manager, Don Revie, was putting me straight into the team to play Leicester City on the Saturday,' Hartford told me. Revie was desperate to reclaim the old First Division title after two runners-up finishes and Hartford was going to be key to the effort. Even so, the player wasn't sure where he'd fit in the all-star XI of Billy Bremner, Johnny Giles, Peter Lorimer, Eddie Gray and the rest.

'I trained with the guys on the Friday and afterwards they made me wear the yellow jersey for being the crappest. I even got my hair cut to club stipulations – it was too long for Don's liking. And then he said: "Just one more thing – the medical."

'I remember having my barium meal and two medics squinting at the X-ray and one saying to the other: 'That's it there – look.' But it was the day of the game in my hotel, the Queens next to the railway station, that Don told me about the hole in my heart. I was stunned. The Leicester players had just arrived for their pre-match lunch and I'll never forget that Tom Jones was milling about reception. 'Sorry,' Don said, 'but your transfer's off.' Then he burst into tears.

'Driving back to West Brom I was all over the radio news. I thought I'd better call home and stopped at a payphone but couldn't get through to Clydebank. By the time I could speak to my mum and dad they'd been told I had cancer. By the time I reached my girl-friend a reporter had wormed his way into her parents' house.

'The next week was crazy, a huge drama. I was moved into a hotel in a bid to shake off the press. Every expert had their say. The top heart specialist in the Midlands was adamant the hole would have no effect on my playing career, effectively contradicting the Leeds doctors. My old team-mates were full of jokes: 'That'll be you here for ever now. They'll build a stand around you.' Back playing with them at Notts Forest I was met by an army of photographers. I suppose they were expecting me to drop down dead.'

He didn't, of course. There would be more to Hartford as a foot-baller – ten clubs after WBA and 50 Scotland caps – but also more to him than football. The rolled-up copy of *Private Eye* he carried into the Preston coffee shop was the first clue to that. Soon he was telling me: 'I'm pretty sure Dad was a Commie. Jock Smith, the school jannie in Clydebank, definitely was.' Politically aware, he animatedly speculated on president-in-waiting Donald Trump, Vladimir Putin and the likely agenda of their first power breakfast together. He mentioned his friend, the BBC journalist, and his other friend, the top trade unionist.

Hartford is proper Lion Rampant royalty. Tartan elite. Picked by The Doc, Wee Willie and Ally with his army, he then survived Argentina – and a bubble perm – to be selected by Big Jock* as well. He enjoyed close-up views of Archie Gemmill's wonder goal, Joe Jordan's handball and David Narey's toe-poke. He played twice in the Maracanã, six times against England and achieved a treasured Wembley double. And he continued Scotland's fine pocket-battleship tradition of tiny, tenacious midfielders, wee guys with big – yes – hearts.

That's the point David Coleman was trying to make in commentary during the 1978 World Cup match against Peru when he described Hartford as 'wholehearted' then quickly thought he should apologise. But the man didn't want anyone's sympathy. As we've learned since, the condition is more common than it first appeared.

Annoyingly I find myself asking Hartford, in the wake of him being dubbed the 'hole-in-the-heart footballer' – 'How did it feel?' This is a standard line of enquiry now for not just sob-sister telly schmaltz but straight-up news programmes. Everyone these days is more than happy to emote; in 1971 it wasn't the done thing, not least among stoic Scottish footballers. But the question seems a reasonable one for Hartford: he was, or so it seemed at the time, a unique case. He might have thought himself a bit of a freak. He could have feared for his health, never mind his career, and the psychological help which exists today wasn't around for him.

'It was a long time ago but a shattering blow? No. I mean, it was confusing and a worry for everyone around me, but footballers are pragmatic fellows. I'm from Clydebank, don't forget, not California. I knew I was fit. Just before going up to Leeds I'd run three miles round a golf course. In the cross-countrys at West Brom I never finished further back than fourth. Leeds told me I'd need an operation. Well, I'm still here and the surgery hasn't been required. I see a cardiologist once a year and the last time he looked at the hole,

---

* Scotland bosses Tommy Docherty, Willie Ormond, Ally MacLeod and Jock Stein.

which hadn't got any bigger, he said: "That's not about to kill you."'

Hartford's Wembulee triumphs were 1977 and 1981. In the first he supplied the heat-seeking delivery for Gordon McQueen to climb as high as the old Twin Towers for a thundering headed goal. In the second, though, he suffered a dislocated elbow. This was a more free-and-easy age for football and the stricken Hartford was able to be met at the tunnel by his union official chum, Jim Mowatt, down from the stands, who proceeded to tag along with the player and remain in the changing room for Stein's half-time team talk.

That wasn't the end of the informalities: 'I was lying on a bench, white as a sheet, as the team doctor was trying to pop my elbow back in place. He couldn't, it was going to be the hospital for me, but neither of our physios wanted to leave the game – we were playing the Auld Enemy, after all – so Jim jumped in the back of the ambulance with me. I had my arm put in a sling and we returned to Wembley to collect my gear. The final whistle had gone and 100,000 folk were streaming out of the stadium. Our cabbie didn't fancy trying to battle through them so he dropped us some way back.' While today's footballers go to great lengths to avoid contact with their public, our hero swam against the roaring tide. 'When these Tartan Army lads spotted me they rushed over. 'Fuckin' brilliant, wee man!' I was in agony after all the hugs but didn't care.'

24

'My first taste of alcohol, almost-black industrial descaler, disgusting and beautiful'

FOOTBALL ON CHRISTMAS DAY

On Christmas Day 1971 there were wise men and there were not-so-wise men. Curmudgeonly, crabbit men and lost and lonely men. Men who viewed this day as an English festival and men for whom it had been just another working day, not so many years before. Men who simply had to get out of the house and men who'd always worshipped a greater God, so of course they would be in this place, drawn by brilliant illumination on the epic march, but with no donkeys to transport them, or municipal omnibuses.

A total of 25,145 men formed this procession. As the Bible says: 'Lo, the star, which they saw in the east, went before them.' It was shining over Easter Road, in reality four stars in one, each affixed to a tall metal pylon. When the men reached the source of the light, the Good Book continues, there was 'exceeding great joy'.

Football on Christmas Day. It couldn't happen now. It won't happen ever again. The Yuletide celebration seems to have been stretched, like a cracker with an elastic band in the middle, over a full month – in much the same way as 'my birthday week'. But there's no room at the inn for football any more.

Christmas Day games were an English tradition for a long time, no matter when 25 December fell, with the clubs reversing the fixtures on Boxing Day for turkey sandwich seconds. In Scotland, there would only be matches when Christmas was a Saturday, which at first glance might suggest that Christmas was doing football a favour and every so often draping tinsel round it. But the opposite was true: football was the sacred thing, unbudgeable in the grand scheme. When Christmas came along and happened to fall on a Saturday, the real day of days, it had to abide by football's rituals.

In England, kick-offs would often be 11 a.m. so most fans could be home in time to resume the festivities, but in Scotland it was 3 p.m. as normal – proper hard-core. And when England stopped putting out a full Christmas Day card in 1959, Scotland carried on doing it. The next time Crimbo was a Saturday – in 1965 – Hibernian were ruthlessly dispatched to Aberdeen and Brechin City all the way to Stranraer. Meanwhile Brechin's Angus neighbours Forfar Athletic slunk back up the road from England after an 8–1 massacre at Berwick which still stands as the wee Rangers' biggest-ever win. Merry bloody Christmas.

When did Christmas get so gigantic and all-enveloping? When did we start feeling self-conscious if we weren't wearing an ironically naff fairy-lights jumper from the beginning of December onwards? When did we start feeling like we were trapped in a snow globe or drowning in a giant Starbucks limited-edition egg nog latte with gingerbread sprinkles or stuck in a lift with some silly posh people from a Richard Curtis movie all rushing to buy a Fortnum & Mason festive hamper?

In 1971, in Scotland at least, Christmas was celebrated more quietly but there were still hazards. Sherry-fumed kisses from maiden aunts with hairy moles on upper lips. Brussels sprouts, marzipan, any present bearing the K-Tel hallmark which would invariably malfunction or fall to pieces. Obligations to perform at family parties, your magic tricks lacking the sleight of hand of the high commissioner of 'Hey presto!' David Nixon, and annoying cousins easily rumbling them. Excitement turning to tiredness turning to fighting turning to tears, although in the middle of the afternoon dutiful silence was demanded because the Queen was speaking to the nation. And in 1971 Bonnie Langford scweamed and scweamed to the nation in a 'special festive edition' of *Junior Showtime*, that grim parade of shockingly confident middle-class brats who didn't have to be shoved centre stage, whose conjuring was always successful and whose top hats might not even have been props.

It was a day of excess missing a certain something: joyful yet dismal, momentous yet lacking deeper meaning. Football! And then, at precisely the moment HRH solemnly intoned on BBC1 and Langford imperilled the special-occasion crystal on STV, 17 games got under way and countrywide 103,134 Scots thought this to be a miracle.

My father and I sneaked out to Easter Road for Hibs vs Rangers and I still don't know how. Even in sexist 1971 where adverts were tag-lined 'Simple enough for a woman to drive' and 'Keep her where she belongs', we were seriously skiving, leaving preparation of the meal and everything else to Mum. Still, it felt thrilling, secretive and dangerous crossing the deserted city to be at the football that day, like we were among the only 25,145 people in the world who knew about the match, where it was happening, how to behave.

We behaved differently. Games between Hibs and Rangers had begun to get edgy on the terraces. Out of sympathy for the Irish Troubles, one lot chanted for the Loyalist paramilitaries while the other sang about crashing rifles, flashing bayonets and the Thompson gun – and empty half-bottles of whisky flew across the sky along with the toilet rolls (non-luxury, sandpaper-like, nicked from public loos). But in 1971 there was a Christmas Day truce, just like in the trenches of the First World War, and football was played.

The rival fans stood side by side, congratulated themselves on escaping the hellish exultation and passed round cans of beer. Some had left behind empty houses so this game was pioneering social service, providing a refuge for lonesome souls long before Christmas jingle 'n' mingle soup kitchens became commonplace.

'Compliments of the season, son – get this down yez,' growled a man in a red-white-and-blue nearly-leather car coat, handing me a tin. The coat was quite something, the Govan riposte to the tedious Yuletide jumper. The beer was quite something, too. My father took the first sip, possibly to check it wasn't piss. Then I tried it. The absence of sweetness or any remote similarity to American cream soda or Creamola Foam was hugely disconcerting. For a brief moment I thought I might be sick until I was able to steady myself. Aged 14, this was a timid step along the road to adulthood: my first taste of alcohol, almost-black industrial descaler, both disgusting and beautiful.

Everyone shared, everyone insisted on it. The scene was incredibly touching. Carry-outs were bigger because it was Christmas, slabs of 24 heaved on to the slopes, the men doing the jobs of beasts of burden. For gold, frankincense and myrrh, read Tartan Special, McEwan's Export, Piper Ale – plus bottles of buzzy Eldorado wine to wash it all down.

But these were the only concessions to the day at Easter Road or any of the other grounds back in no-crib-for-a-bed '71. No one wore Santa hats, there were no yule logs at the pie stands and – if you were lucky – just a smattering of cartoon snow on the covers of the match programmes.

Holly twisted round the O of 'Official' would have been deemed decadent, a sure sign that the goose was getting fatter; that the custom of loosening trouser top buttons post-feast would soon commence; that a department store chain's festive commercials would one day be regarded as 'events'; that you'd eventually know more people who got an entire fortnight off work at Christmas than those who didn't; that the dreaded Curtis would ultimately do his worst and make *Love Actually*.

Sadly, Scottish football got lost in the avalanche of 'superChristmastasticness' and the games stopped. But John Knox, outlawer of Yule in the 16th century, would surely have been proud of the players who participated in those matches, running around energetically in short sleeves, and the chittering fans who watched them, warmed by outsize fake sheepskin collars and all that bevvy.

And the word was indomitable.

In the Easter Road Nativity, Rangers assumed the role of Herod. Battered for 89 minutes, they stole victory at the death. Their fans, normally triumphalist, offered Dad and me condolences, good tidings and yet more cans.

25

'Baldy! Baldy!'

THE FOLLICLY CHALLENGED

In the hit parade of casual fan abuse, the young female police officer got it the worst. Patrolling the pitch in her squeaky new AirWairs, walking right round its perimeter, she would arrive back at the rowdiest enclosure with creeping dread, for every rendition would be louder than the one before, eventually reaching a Last Night of the Proms level of bellowing and gusto: 'GET IT UP YOU WHILE YOU'RE YOUNG! GET IT UH-HUP YOU WHILE YOU'RE YOUNG!'

Spare a thought, though, for the follicly-challenged footballer. WPCs were eventually removed from the firing line at games, without having to wait for the #MeToo revolution, but who was censoring the ridiculing of the slap-headed, chrome-domed, denuded, unadorned, tonsured, glabrescent as a coot, completely hairless full-back?

'BALDY! BALDY!'

Or maybe not completely hairless. Maybe the full-back – stuck on the touchline, easy to pick off – had tried to make a little go a long way, growing his last remaining strands to hippie length then, one side to the other, like a nervous rookie boatman in charge of the landing ropes for the first time, throwing and hoping.

Drew Jarvie was one of the cleverest footballers in Scotland. Before 'ten' was more than just a number, and signified stealth and surprise, Jarvie was that man at both Airdrie and Aberdeen. But he could contrive all the shapeshifting he liked, make all the ghosting runs he liked. Opposition fans would spot his shiny heid a mile off.

'BALDY! BALDY!'

'Och, I had a comb-over,' he chuckled. 'I wanted to get what little hair I had cut right off but my wife and daughter wouldn't let me. "Don't worry, it's fine," they said. When I look back at old photos I just cringe.

'A blustery day at Montrose or Brechin and the barnet would be flying everywhere. Pittodrie did me no favours with that wee wind tunnel down in the corner. And then there was Arbroath right by the North Sea, always blowing a gale, the only ground in the world where you need to check the shipping forecast before kick-off – absolutely horrendous.'

The Gayfield gusts would cause games to be abandoned and the adjacent Pleasureland surely missed a trick not switching to wind power for their dodgems and merry mixers. 'Bobby Charlton and Ralph Coates had comb-overs but I don't think they ever had to play at places like that,' continued Jarvie. 'The worst for abuse, though, for non-stop shouting, always the same thing, were Ibrox and Parkhead.'

'BALDY! BALDY!'

'Fans can pick on the smallest thing and be relentless,' said St Johnstone's Henry Hall, just as crafty an old-school inside-forward as Jarvie and just as gleaming on top. 'When I wasn't being called "Baldy" it was "Big nose", so, aye, maybe not always the smallest thing.

'I maintain that every time after scoring a goal when I ran back to halfway my captain Benny Rooney would ruffle my hair really vigorously and that's why I ended up losing it. I admit to copying Bobby Charlton with the comb-over but the style, if you can call it that, did absolutely nothing for my long-range shooting.'

Meanwhile Hibernian's Pat Stanton sauntered around with his *Thunderbirds* hair and, rocking another killer parting, Dundee's John Duncan resembled one of those male models on the covers of knitting patterns. Both were handsome, thick of thatch, untroubled, glued down.

And then there was Alfie Conn when he was at Rangers, surely the possessor of the most ostentatious locks in all Scottish football. Think Charles II (1630–85) and those bangs. Imagine Deep Purple as the house band for the king's court. Then visualise Conn striding into the royal long room and, with the merest of flicks of his gigantic tresses, scattering the assembly like bagatelle.

Jarvie will fess up to some vanity: 'I bought this spray which was "guaranteed" to keep the strands in place but it never worked. They were uncontrollable and [Dons team-mate] Neale Cooper, with his fine head of curls, used to tease me about them. He'd say: "Drew wasn't offside there but unfortunately his hair was."'

At least some supporters would try for humour rather than the standard greeting when there was a billiard-ball bonce in their midst. Eamonn Bannon of Dundee United was winding up for a shy against Hibernian when an Easter Road wag quipped: 'Mind ye dinnae throw yer heid in!'

These theatres of cruelty might have been raucous with baldist baiting during the 1970s but almost a century before, Arbroath goalkeeper Ned Doig was so self-conscious about his lack of hair that he always wore a cap held in place with elastic. Opposing centre-forwards would sometimes twang the band to annoy him and local lore has it that if ever one of those notorious gales which battered the Angus coast exposed his pate, Doig would give chase to the hat before the ball.

'BALDY! BALDY!'

Bald goalies even more than bald full-backs have had no hiding place from the taunts, especially lower down the divisions in grounds tight to the pitch, with enough quiet moments for the fans who believed they possessed the pithy wit of Noël Coward, and were possibly under the assumption they'd struck up a stunningly original chant. Clydebank's Jim Gallacher amassed a grand total of 738 games and so must have endured the taunting more than almost anyone else. 'It was relentless,' he said. 'I couldn't just wander into the centre circle to get away. And even if the shouts were coming from fat guys with teeth missing and maybe bloody awful perms or crap highlights I just had to take them. And the better I played the worse it would get.'

If you're thinking the jibe to be an old one which has since died out, then Alex Gogić who arrived at Hamilton Accies in 2017 was astonished to hear it during the warm-up before his debut at Hearts. 'I'm Greek-Cypriot so no one knew me or that I shaved my head. What is this hang-up Scottish people have for a man who shows no hair?'

For Jarvie, Hall and others who braved the abuse, the shave-it-all-off fad came too late. As did hair transplant technology. As did the roll calls of football's greatest bald players where our men could at least have enjoyed some kinship with the likes of Zinedine Zidane, Fabien Barthez, Yordan Letchkov, Esteban Cambiasso* and the rest.

Yes, they were baldies but they were also indomitable.

* Scorer of football's greatest-ever goal, the conclusion of a 24-pass move involving nine Argentina players vs Serbia & Montenegro in the 2006 World Cup. Glorious Esteban.

26

''Cause every little thing gonna be all right'

WHEN DIXIE DEANS
MET BOB MARLEY

Hopefully you've got the idea by now that Scottish football is not to be underestimated, that it is entirely possible for Bob Marley in a crowded room to identify Dixie Deans as the most famous person present, rather than the other way around. So here's the question: was the near-spherical centre-forward the inspiration for the reggae king's 'Redemption Song'?

Was the track, indeed, a tribute to Deans's indomitability?

In between Celtic's European Cup triumph and the emergence of the Quality Street Gang, Jock Stein recruited players from other Scottish clubs who ensured continued dominance at home even if the team couldn't quite replicate the glory of Lisbon.

If you were being really unkind – if you were a Rangers fan – you might describe this intake as less Quality Street, more a bag of Revels. Harry Hood came from Clyde, Tom Callaghan from Dunfermline Athletic, Johnny Doyle from Ayr United and then there was Deans who weeble-wobbled along the old A74 from Motherwell. Dixie had the name of a goal grabber – actually the nickname, taken from the Everton legend – and the mean-critter moustache evoking the Wild West and its hired guns. He certainly riddled the Hibernian defence with holes and couldn't stop scoring hat-tricks against them. The most famous act of his career was his goal in the 1972 Scottish Cup final when he dumped three Hibee internationalists on their backsides as he moseyed into their box with rootin', tootin' intent. Three sets of spurs glinted and turned a few more revolutions before halting in sad unison while desperado Deans strode off with yet more notches on his gun. Well, not so much strode as attempted a somersault, possibly the most risible in the history of goal celebrations.

But the tumble wasn't actually Dixie's most notorious act. This came ten days previously in Celtic's European Cup semi-final against Inter Milan. Nil–nil like the first leg, the tie went to penalty kicks, still a flashy new procedure for settling continental competition, and the first time for these teams, with Deans opening proceedings. Stein checked if he was ready. 'Aye, boss,' came the reply.

'Of course I had to walk from the halfway line to take the kick, something I hadn't considered beforehand,' Deans told me. 'That took forever. It felt like I was wearing diving boots. I broke into a wee jog then stopped. I got really self-conscious. It was the longest, hardest walk of my life.'

The 75,000 crowd, sensing his nervousness, fell silent. They didn't know how to respond, not having witnessed a shoot-out before, and Dixie didn't know how to walk without feeling like he was indeed in a cowboy movie, only this time it was 50–50 that he could be the one chewing lead at the end. Do not forsake him, oh my darling.

'There was mud on the ball so I wiped it off,' Deans recalled. 'I was going to hit it low to their goalie's left but he moved so I lifted it.' Over the bar and, in legend, over the Parkhead roof and the furthest multi-storey flats. 'I didn't actually miss by much but because it kept on rising there were cartoons in the papers the next day about the Apollo 16 astronauts orbiting the Moon informing Mission Control: "Tell Dixie we've found his ball."'

Rangers fans loved this. That same night across Glasgow they'd won through to the Cup Winners' Cup final while their rivals were discovering a new and horrible way of losing. They would have witnessed Deans's calamity in the highlights on chip shop TVs while queueing for their white pudding suppers.

The penalty-kick fall guy was big news. Driving home, Deans turned into his street to find reporters clustered on the doorstep. He sped off and went into hiding, drowning his sorrows in a hotel, only to be flushed out by the *Daily Express* the following day with a photograph cropped to paint a picture of desolation and excommunication. The headline read: 'Dixie Deans – the loneliest man in the world.'

But he wasn't lonely at Hampden. The bulk of that 110,000 cup final crowd wanted to embrace him, or at least make a decent effort at extending arms round his magnificent road-compressor frame. Then, a few years later, when he was winding up in Australia with Adelaide City, one of the most important musical figures of the 20th century sought an audience with him to ask: 'Are you the Dixie Deans who played for Celtic?'

Deans in response could not have asked: 'Are you the Bob Marley who played with the Wailers, popularised reggae and was one tremendously cool and laid-back dude, never more so than when swaggering down a dingy back alley with your gang in a famous photograph, flight cases containing guitars or possibly rifles plus many attachments?' And the reason he couldn't ask this was that he'd never actually heard of Marley.

He was unnerved by the musician's dreadlocks. 'His hair was long, matted together and quite frankly looked in need of a bloody good wash.' So he was surprised by Marley's football knowledge, even more his Celtic obsession. 'Bob said: "I'm a big fan. I know all about Jock Stein. I'd love to go to Scotland and kick a ball about Celtic Park."' Deans was just as impressed by Marley's football ability when the musician joined in an Adelaide City training session. History doesn't record whether the pair discussed Deans's penalty miss, or whether Marley lamented not being at the Inter game when he could have run on to the pitch and handed Dixie a giant spliff for 'medical purposes' during the fateful walk to the painted spot on the ground. Okay, maybe 'Redemption Song' wasn't a Dixie tribute. Possibly, as Marley's swansong, knowing his days were numbered as he battled skin cancer, this poignant track should be read as the story of his life, from poverty to greatness. Nevertheless, Deans's determination to shrug off his misfortune to poach goals with even greater intent against hapless Hibs must have impressed his famous admirer.

The story of this improbable encounter amused for a while and then it was forgotten about. Fast-forward several years when Rangers were booted down to the bottom tier of Scottish football following the club's financial implosion. Feeling sorry for themselves, the fans sought comfort in another Marley song, 'Three Little Birds'. 'Don't worry about a thing,' the supporters chorused, ''cause every little thing gonna be all right.'

But then they remembered the Dixie connection with its composer. 'Hang on: the guy we used to mock for being fat, for never scoring in an Old Firm game, for having to play for Celtic despite growing up a bluenose, for that penalty howler, was a hero to Boaby Marley, our new court minstrel? …

'Get that bloody record aff!'

27

'I was given away as a baby,
passed right doon the street'

KENNY BURNS AND
GEORGE GRAHAM, THE
TOUGHEST OF STARTS

George Graham and Kenny Burns missed sharing the Scotland dressing room by a season, which is a shame, as they would surely have had stories to swap about how hugely unpromising starts in life had been overcome to reach the pinnacle of a bagpipe-skirling Hampden debut.

Mind you, the conversation could have got competitive and, particularly with Burns involved, comical. They might have tried to outdo each other's hardship, rather like Monty Python in that sketch about a group of self-made bores all claiming to have had the humblest of beginnings which ends: 'Hole in the ground, you say? We got evicted from ours ...'

Gorgeous George could have begun: 'When I was a boy every single item of clothing was a hand-me-down and every single thing was patched.'

And Burns Unit could have countered: 'Ah, but when I was a boy what did I play with? There was an old car in our garden, a Ford Prefect. I used to drive it six yards forwards then six yards back. Hours of endless fun.'

Gorgeous George again: 'One of my duties was following horses round the village, picking up their shite.'

Burns Unit: 'My brothers won me a bicycle playing cards down the pub. It was a lassie's one, pink with rainbow tassels on the handlebars and a basket. Still, it got me further than those six yards.'

None of this is boring and all of it is true. Both started out as strikers, realised there was too much running involved, so Graham became a midfielder nicknamed Stroller and Burns a defender who tackled with extreme prejudice. Burns won a European Cup and Graham a Double, then further honours as a manager. Not bad for two guys who had so little going for them virtually from day one.

In Bargeddie, North Lanarkshire, Graham's father died three weeks after he was born, while 15 miles to the west in Glasgow's Priesthill, Burns was 'given away as a wee baby, passed right doon the street'.

Graham didn't know his father while Burns didn't know his mother, father or stepfather. But he had the woman who took him in when others wouldn't or couldn't and Graham had a big brother manning up at 16 who he would come to call his dad. In one sense these two seemed to have nothing; in another their formative years didn't lack anything, least of all love.

Wrapped in swaddling in September 1953, Burns was offered at every doorstep in Priesthill's Peat Road. He knows the journey travelled was 500 yards because he measured it out later. Five hundred yards of rejections? He didn't see it like that. 'The woman who gave birth to me had lots of kids already and couldn't cope with another,' he told me. 'Maybe it was the same story at the other houses and they were full up.' And as if to emphasise his faith in community he points out that he didn't quite have to leave Peat Road to find a new home.

And a new name. 'Mrs Burns, who became Mum to me and who I thought the world of, took me in. Mary Burns, always in her pinny, always with a fag.' Ma Burns's large family of her own was no impediment, with young Kenny having to fight to be heard among four brothers and three sisters. He remembers her accidentally lighting her fags with ten bob notes and the brothers leaping across the kitchen to stop her. He remembers her asking him to buy a pan loaf and him cheekily demanding threepence to run the errand which brought a clout on the ear from his siblings – 'Never charge your mother for anything.' And he can't forget, at ten years old, being taken to the 'big room' to be told she'd died.

She never saw Burns play, but maybe he wouldn't have got his big chance in football without her. He's never tried to trace his birth mother, out of respect. 'Everyone's into their family trees, aren't they? But if I did that I think it would be disloyal to the wonderful woman who brought me up,' he said.

Graham's father Robert died on Christmas Day 1944 from tuberculosis. Like Burns, he hasn't been curious to find out who his dad was. Emerging from the war, families dealt with their own tragedies stoically, and this was especially true in the west of Scotland. The hippy hadn't been invented, far less the neo-hippy, always on a 'journey', permanently in touch with one's 'feelings'. Feelings in the world of Burns and Graham stayed locked up, like a matron's sherry cabinet, and a typical journey would have been a trip to the outside loo or a trek to find work.

Like Burns, Graham was the baby of a large brood, seven kids in total, although one of his three sisters would also succumb to TB. The eldest child who became the father of the house left school to labour on a farm in Ayrshire and send money home. Graham never called Andy 'Dad' but that was his brother's role. When clubs began courting Graham, they would have to persuade Andy they would be right for the talented youngster.

While Graham's mother Janet worked on local farms, the children were responsible for growing the vegetables for the pot, the soup having to sustain the family all week. The procedure for keeping potatoes going right through the harshest winters – 'A layer of hay, soil, then more hay' – is burned on his memory. Boys don't forget such information. As the Jesuits almost said: 'Give me a child until he is seven and able to recite his mother's Co-operative Society membership number and I will show you the man.'

Graham has never forgotten his roots but would go on to develop a taste for the finer things in life, and after bringing suaveness to the dugout would be invited to model menswear for the luxury label Aquascutum. I asked him what was the most he'd ever spent on clobber and at first he wouldn't say, possibly not wanting to appear boastful, but then came the admission about two pairs of shoes: 'British leather but Italian-made – it has to be Italian – a thousand quid.'

Burns would need the fatherly influence and moral guidance of Brian Clough at Nottingham Forest, albeit that much of it was eccentric, such as when the player found himself at a flower show with his boss, down among the sweet peas – surely the moment of peak incongruity for any studs-sharpened hardman of the game. Graham appeared to be a ready-made managerial success at Arsenal, not requiring anyone's help, but some of that guidance wouldn't have gone amiss when a bung scandal got him sacked, though maybe not from Cloughie as mentor.*

Both men achieved great things and are a credit to those they called 'Mum' and 'Dad' and who helped make them indomitable. Burns revisits Peat Road often, sometimes to pace out those 500 yards, or just to stand at the spot where for him there was room at the inn. 'One time this old fella came up to me and said: "Are you Kenny Burns?" "Aye," I said, "but the fantastic woman who lived there knew me as Kenneth."'

Graham is similarly in awe of brother Andy. 'Becoming the father of that house was some responsibility for a lad of 16,' he said. 'Andy went down the mines later which would have been tough. Eventually he got a family of his own and proved himself a great dad for real. He died a few years ago but I speak to his widow Babs all the time. I never felt deprived because I didn't know my actual father. I had

* In 1993 former Tottenham Hotspur chairman Alan Sugar told the High Court that Clough 'likes a bung'.

Andy and that was brilliant. I hope my actual father would have been proud of me making it all the way to the Scotland team but I know Andy was and that's enough. He was a great guy and my hero.'

28

'My boys are professional sportsmen,
not performing seals – how dare you!'

THE GREATEST
FOOTBALL SONG

Bill Martin looked out of the plane window and thought he was about to die. Propellers! The bloody thing had propellers! Why on earth had he let Rod Stewart talk him into travelling to the 1974 World Cup in West Germany in the rock star's private jet?

Bring your brother, Stewart said – one hundred and eighty quid for you both. 'Everyone on board seemed to have a brother,' Martin recalled. 'Rod with his brother Bob, Junior Campbell with his brother Tom, and me with Ian. But I was the one sweating buckets and shouting at Rod. How was this stupid contraption going to get into the air and stay there?'

Bing-bong, Caledonian pop royalty. Campbell was the singer with Marmalade,* Rod was Rod, and Martin was one half of Britain's most successful songwriting duo, panicking like mad. 'I couldn't help thinking about Buddy Holly, the Big Bopper and Ritchie Valens crashing in their plane. But, bloody hell, the newspapers writing up this tragedy-waiting-to-happen were bound to get my name wrong, weren't they? They'd have mixed me up with Bob Martin, the dog

---

* Marmalade's 'Reflections of My Life' is the greatest song Rod Stewart never recorded.

guy. You know, "Bob Martin Wormer Tablets".'

It wasn't supposed to be like this. Four years before, England should have won the World Cup and 'Back Home', the song Martin penned with choonsmith sidekick Phil Coulter, would have remained on top of the Hit Parade for the rest of 1970. 'I'd have probably got a knighthood,' he sighed. And been able to afford his own plane, one without need of propellers. But Sir Alf Ramsey blundered with a substitution and in Mexico's thin air a goalkeeper possibly nicknamed Tiddles clawed at a looping header like it was a ball of wool and missed. England crashed out. 'After that we couldn't even give away the records as ashtrays.'

Martin when we met was funny, crabbit, blustering, no respecter of reputations and, like Sir Alex Ferguson, a fully paid-up member of the Govan Hall of Fame. He co-authored the UK's first triumph at the Eurovision Song Contest with 'Puppet on a String' and those stack-heeled stompers of the tartan tyranny of the Bay City Rollers. And, he insisted, 'Back Home' was the very first football song. Hang on, wasn't it 'World Cup Willie', the 1966 ditty written and sung by Lonnie Donegan, who was of course another Scot? 'That was a piece of rubbish!' he snorted. 'And Lonnie didn't like to let on that he came from Glasgow. He cultivated a cockney image.'

Martin is big on authenticity. Regarding Ramsey: 'He was a cockney who pretended to be posh.' The manager was horrified by 'Back Home', the entire concept. 'Terry Venables told Alf that Phil and I wanted the players to sing it. "I'll shoot that down in flames," he said. I went to see Alf. He said: "My boys are elite sportsmen, not performing seals – how dare you!" I knew he had a brother who was a big drinker so I said: "Well, your brother thought it was a great idea in the pub last night ..."'

'Back Home' may have been a straightforward oompah-ish number with a routine surge of key change in the middle but the idea of footballers singing anywhere other than in the communal bath also struggled to gain acceptance from the music establishment. Its creator, though, was determined. He was indomitable. 'We had to get the song past [BBC Head of Light Entertainment] Bill Cotton, who didn't know a crotchet from a hatchet and only got that job because his father was [bandleader, "Wakey Wakey" radio star] Billy Cotton,' said Martin. 'I persuaded Tony Lewis who was Shirley Bassey's agent to play it to him because he was so jealous of songwriters that I'd have been thrown out of his office. The demo was me singing and Phil on piano, only my partner had to play one-handed as he'd been on the hooly the night before and had fallen over. "That sounds like a guy with a broken arm," said Bill. He was dead right. So maybe he wasn't as cloth-eared as we thought.'

Martin and Coulter decided the team anthem should be 'like a war song'. It took half an hour to bash out, which was standard for them. 'The hand-clapping at the start we copied from the football terraces. My wife's godfather was Kenneth Wolstenholme and he wanted us to include his "They think it's all over" from the commentary in 1966. "No way," I said. Otherwise we'd have had to give him royalties.'

Eventually Martin was allowed to meet the England team who seemed unimpressed by his Tin Pan Alley credentials. He was in awe of the players, though, and maybe that was the problem. 'You've got to remember I'd been a footballer. Okay, I'd once had a trial with Partick Thistle. Okay, when I claimed to have played for Rangers it was really Johannesburg Rangers. I wasn't getting anywhere with flattery so decided to go on the offensive. "You, Bobby Moore, you play at snail speed!" "Alan Ball, you run around like a headless chicken!" I was talking football and they were listening. I told them the song would make them money, which always impresses footballers, and that I'd guarantee them *Top of the Pops* and a gold record.'

'Back Home' was recorded at Pye Studios. Ball, famously likened by Jim Baxter to the helium-voiced entertainer Jimmy Clitheroe, surprised Martin by being able to hold a tune. Jeff Astle was probably the best singer. Only two 'takes' were required and the single flew off the racks, shifting 100,000 copies a day. The players made it on to *TOTP*, performing in dinner suits, making them easily the most stuffed-shirt, boringly dressed act in the entire history of the show. But they loved being pop stars, Martin loved hanging out with them and over in Mexico he really wanted them to win the World Cup. 'I may be Scottish but this was business.'

By 1974 the tradition of Scots acting as musical fluffers for England swanning off to World Cups was over – the whiteshirts' place at the tournament had been taken by the boys in dark blue. Martin survived the flight to West Germany then made other arrangements to get home. But he got his own back on Stewart at a big party in Frankfurt to commemorate Scotland's glorious failure in exiting unbeaten. 'Rod and Billy Connolly were there along with some other famous folk and the manager, Willie Ormond, asked if I could get one of them to perform for the team. Billy said: "Get lost, I do this all the time; I'm here to relax." Rod's excuse was: "Sorry, but I'd need an orchestra." Bloody prima donnas. I got up on stage: "I'd like to introduce Scotland's greatest-ever entertainer ..." I could see Billy putting his head in his hands while Rod was shuffling towards the exit. I'd already spotted World Cup Willie himself so I went: "... Of course, ladies and gentlemen, and absolutely without question, it's the one-and-only – sorry, Billy, no way, Rod – Lonnie Donegan!"'

In the World Cup of Scotland serenading England, Martin claimed a stunning victory with 'Back Home' and rated it the greatest three and a half minutes of his illustrious career. Its success sparked plenty of requests from football clubs for songs but neither he nor Coulter was interested. 'We'd already written the best. Why would I have wanted to work for Crystal Palace or Heart of bloody Midlothian? For Christ's sake, we're professionals!'

29

'One Tillicoultry, there's only one Tillicoultry'

DOUGIE DONNELLY,
SOFA SO GOOD

They're just so smooth. Smoothing their way across the continent. Smoothing from private planes to blacked-out wagons and on to sound stages. Smoothing through the read-throughs with only the teensiest rewrites required ('Didn't I pass the ball to Leo last time? Maybe this time he should pass to *me*.'). And then they're ready. The world's greatest – Leo and Cristiano, plus Neymar and Salah and Mbappé and Lewandowski – are shooting another commercial.

What will it be like? Oh, inspiring, probably, like all the ones before. And inclusive, mustn't forget that. In the editing suite the players will look on quizzically as ordinary people in dreary clothes are green-screened on to the sidelines. Then the final touch-ups ('Speed me up there, please ... Didn't you catch my rabona? ... So my hair looks fantastic, guys, yes?') before our football gods smooth their way back to the airport for espressos in the VIP lounge and huggy goodbyes.

'See you in Milan next Tuesday for Rolex.'

'No, man, I'm doing Mastercard that day. Dubai, world's tallest building.'

'But Mastercard's a week on Thursday in Paris?'

'Ah no, this is Mastercard *Super Elite* ...'

This is the smooth life of the game's icons who are basically selling their own magnificence and in ads will never have to wear outsized car oil filters (Pat Jennings), munch crisps (Gary Lineker), share a shower with a bashed-nosed boxer (Kevin Keegan), admit to dandruff (Joe Hart) or go for a pizza with other sad, loser penalty flunkers (Gareth Southgate, Stuart Pearce, Chris Waddle). The icons won't do anything naff to shift product. English (and Irish) footballers will only get to make a few bob from advertising if they do.

But what about the Scottish game's most marketable? What can they flog? Kenny Dalglish, Graeme Souness and Alan Hansen were once our biggest stars and, rather like how they grabbed the European Cup after a Wembley triumph and tried to scarper with it, this triumvirate vacuumed up many of the ad opportunities. Dalglish was dubbed into Japanese to sell whisky, which possibly made him no less indecipherable to English ears. Souness went with Irn-Bru, which was apt, given that he was also made from girders. And Hansen's dour drollery helped promote, among other things, beer, insurance, a supermarket chain, football pools and Bull Boy Shoes – tragic trainers which can only have been made marginally more attractive to the youth market by the inclusion of free shin pads autographed by the suave defender, though perhaps not sufficiently to disprove the theory, voiced by somebody once, that you win nothing with kids.

Hansen may be the most prolific we've had at goods-and-services enhancement; indeed in his case it could be called 'enhansenment', but he's not the best. The most trusting face and the most persuasive voice do not in fact belong to a player or manager. Step forward, the Doogster.

Dougie Donnelly, who fronted football coverage on the BBC for more than 30 years, lent those comfy, safe, sweetie-wifie tones to an out-of-town furniture store and created a legend – 'Tillicoultry, near Stirling'.

How on earth did he do this? He was only reciting a Scottish place name, after all, and pinpointing it on the map. And not actually as precisely as he could have done. 'There was some confusion on the streets of Stirling,' Donnelly admitted. 'Once a traffic warden marched right up to me with a torn face: "Can you no' say 'near Alloa' instead? It would be a whole lot more accurate because you wouldn't believe the numpties I get pestering me who've got lost trying to buy a new three-piece suite."'

Ah, the gentle lies the ad industry will spin. At the marketing strategy meeting, did a Don Draper-type insist on 'near Stirling' to solidify the name of the client – Sterling, furniture floggers – in consumers' minds? And was he then gifted a top-of-the-range sofa for his corner office (for Scotch at 11 and shagging the secretaries after lunch)?

Well, it was a winning campaign with the right man spearheading it. In and out of football, he'd attempted to sex up his image by compering Miss Scotland beauty contests and, on his short-lived TV chat show, cosying up on a sofa with nudie-book queen Fiona Richmond, only for the entire nation to wince, crying as one: 'Dougie, son, this isnae you!' Letting it all hang out or locking up the church? Donnelly was definitely the latter and after dabbling in the carnal he needed something couthie, eventually finding it just off the A91.

The actor Tom Fleming was the sonorous Scottish voice of many state occasions including royal weddings and funerals and a fine job he did, too – but Fleming never had a catchphrase. Donnelly's followed him everywhere. 'The funniest moment of my career, no doubt about it, came at the 1992 European Championships in Sweden,' he said. 'Scotland were playing the CIS and I was on the TV gantry at Norrköping with Alex McLeish. The Tartan Army were massed directly below us and just as I was about to fire a penetrating question at Big Eck, they all burst into song: "One Tillicoultry, there's only one Tillicoultry!"'

Cristiano, Leo – can you possibly beat that?

30

'Death smiles at us all.
All we can do is smile back'

FRANK HAFFEY SHRUGS OFF
OUR WORST HUMILIATION

The Australian TV drama *Spyforce* seemed perfect for Frank Haffey, goalkeeper-turned-thespian.

After Wembley 1961 and England 9 Scotland 3, maybe it wasn't quite enough that he'd emigrated to the other side of the world in search of a new life where, as an actor, he could pretend to be other people.

Perhaps the extent of the annihilation all but necessitated him being in a show with a theme of invisibility, telling the WWII story of a covert military unit in the South Pacific operating deep behind Japanese lines.

Also in *Spyforce* was young Russell Crowe, not yet a gladiator and superstar. If their paths could have crossed on the show, it's tempting to fantasise about them befriending each other: the man held responsible for the worst result in Scotland's football history and the bloke who would get down to his toga to utter the line: 'Brothers, what we do in life echoes in eternity.' For good measure Crowe's Maximus added: 'Death smiles at us all. All we can do is smile back.'

Yes, you might well imagine that Haffey will have to go into time added on when eternity's done before his desperate afternoon under the old Twin Towers is forgotten. Some four decades later team-mate

Denis Law bumped into him on a trip Down Under when Haffey confided he was thinking about coming back to live in Scotland. 'Don't,' cautioned Law, 'it's still too soon.'

But it's equally true that Haffey – brawny, curly-haired, hand-somely square-jawed – smiled back. He peered at the horrors of that game and grinned. He located the comedy sub-sub-subtext of leaking nine goals which everyone else missed. He chuckled at his own misfortune. 'Well, I had to do something,' he said.

That doyen of Scottish football wordsmiths, Hugh McIlvanney, called the hammering 'a public assassination' and 'our greatest humil-iation in 90 years of international football'. So how exactly did Haffey react? In the dressing room afterwards he burst into song. The Harry Lauder ditties he chose could have included 'The Saftest o' the Family', which goes: 'Nearly all the boys I play wi' try to mak' a fule o' me/They'd mak' you think that two and two were three.' The Wembley tally might have prompted calls for a recount but it was all too accurate. In the communal bath the Lawman again offered with-ering perspective: 'For a goalkeeper, Frank, you're a great singer.'

On the team bus passing the hastily retreating Tartan Army, over-sized tammies no longer jauntily angled but worn with epic self-consciousness as if they were psychedelic cowpats, the players dived under the seats with the exception of Haffey who offered the fans a half-mad grin, like that of a travelling salesman who's been too long on the road with uninspiring merchandise and no takers.

Haffey clearly thought he was on to something with his leer. Before the team left London, he obliged newspaper photographers by reprising it underneath Big Ben. The time on the clock? Well, 9.03 a.m. of course. Then, not wanting the Scottish paparazzi to feel left out when the party arrived back in Glasgow, he posed next to the sign for Central Station's platform nine.

Celebrities today spend small fortunes on damage-limitation PR to firefight for them at times of extreme tabloid discomfort and these guys would be steering their clients far, far away from stunts like this, reasoning there's no positive spin which can be applied to the most goals that have ever flown past a Scottish custodian of the sticks.

But in a more innocent age Haffey must have concluded, all by himself, that the best way for the nation to get over the humiliation was to demonstrate that he hadn't been broken by it. And the best way to do that was to act the big galoot – the big, indomitable galoot.

The gags were always going to come; he'd simply got in there first. 'What's the time?' opposition fans would shout when he turned out for his club Celtic. 'Almost ten past Haffey!' But he insists his story was embellished by others to make it even funnier. For instance, he really did race to meet a wayward corner kick with a firm header but there was a good reason for this: he'd already left his box. The fact he was wearing his bunnet, though, must have made the incident hilarious. In another Celtic game he really did boot a goal kick into his own net but this was because he was still dazed from an earlier collision. And if he continued to take the blows in the Scottish League, without the consolation of a highly remunerative self-mocking advertising contract, then he obviously didn't high-tail it to the far side of the world immediately after Wembley, which the tragic version of his tale claims.

In Oz, as well as acting, Haffey worked as a singer and a comedian. By the time of the doomy 'Number nine, number nine ...' refrain on the Beatles' *White Album*, he was telling jokes to earn a few Aussie dollars.

Veterans of the mirth scene insist Glasgow's Pavilion Theatre is the toughest of all gigs, but surely a Scottish football audience when you've just been pulverised by England and you're viewed as the chief culprit tops that. 'Old folks' homes were the best places to play because the punters couldn't walk out,' Haffey quipped. 'I used to say: "I don't have to be here, you know. I could be at home with the wife. Fighting."' He also ran a goalkeeping clinic on the Gold Coast and, no, that's not another joke.

About the game, the game, the terrible game, those fine, upstanding Englishmen Bobby Robson and Johnny Haynes sympathised with Haffey, insisting that their team had one of those days when every shot flew into the net with the keeper only really being at fault with a couple of the goals. And Sir Alex Ferguson, talking about the Scotland–England rivalry, told me that as a fan at Wembley that day he didn't lambast Haffey; rather, that more than 40 years later he was still raging about the referee allowing a highly dubious Auld Enemy strike to stand when the Scots had got back to 2–3.

In 'Keep Right on to the End of the Road', Harry Lauder sang: 'With a big stout heart to a long steep hill/We may get there with a smile.' Haffey smiled and played the clown and the sumph so that we might feel a bit better about the result, and ourselves.

31

'Erra Protestant macaroon bars!'

FOOTBALL FOOD

Recently, when Heinz were trying to think of a way to squeeze more profit out of baked beans, they hit on the idea of offering them up frozen in microwaveable sandwiches. It didn't sound much like a winner with seriously underwhelmed foodie correspondents deciding there was only one snack which would be less appetising – a waspburger.

That's waspburger as in a bun full of the psychotic dagger-arsed gits. The verdict was the ultimate put-down but a snack based on the *Vespula germanica* is obviously gruesome fantasy. The wider world, though, must know nothing about Alloa Athletic's waspburger, which is a thing, and long may this match-day delicacy stay delightfully esoteric.

So named because Alloa are the Wasps, it's black pudding, potato scone and bacon. Top baldy Supermarionation-spectacled chef Heston Blumenthal would charge upwards of £20 for that devastating combo but it's available for a couple of quid from a Portakabin behind Recreation Park's main stand which commemorates the great John White having graced this ground. Now his successors scuttle and dart in black-and-yellow hoops of a Golden Gordon variety against a backdrop of the heather-clad Ochil Hills, one of the bonniest in all football.

Why do we need food at games? That's a whole other debate but the fact is we have it, and have for a while. Much of football's larder can seem basic, weird, sad, macabre and hilarious, but quirky, customised treats have always been sourced. Such as the waspburger now and, back in the 1970s, the Protestant macaroon bar.

In truth this was an ordinary, non-denominational macaroon bar of the kind sold at most Scottish grounds at the time, but presumably Rangers had the Ibrox faithful believing theirs had been selected with the kind of master-race fascism practised by Waitrose in rooting out misshapen carrots. Maybe the bluenose comedian Lex McLean taste-tested them, with final ratification coming from the Rev. Ian Paisley.

'Erra Protestant macaroon bars!' I heard this vendor's plaintive cry in 1971 during my Ibrox initiation. 'Erra Protestant spearmint gum!' I heard that too. Why were they always sold together, these two – Protestant or regular? Well, why is the future unknowable? Why did the chicken cross the road? Why are all actresses 29 years old? Why does anything exist? Why do birds suddenly appear, every time you are near? Some things just are.

These vendors had the run of the place. Rangers had yet to spot the in-house potential of round, ground meat which could be called a Loyalburger and make them money. Approved club grub sold under the shelter of a stand roof – the equivalent of tea at the Ritz for Govan's hungry hordes – was just a twinkle in the marketing man's eye. Other teams hadn't considered the potential of branded nosh either, so in this unregulated world, brown cardboard boxes were lugged on to terraces in all weathers for the flogging of random snacks, bringing sustenance to the supporters like they were farming rice on stepped paddy fields and the bell had been rung for lunch.

How random? Oh, Chipmunk crisps, Smax biscuits, luncheon meat rolls, ice poles. Stuff you never saw anywhere else. Stuff which must have been nicked from a carry-out in Ceauşescu's Romania. Stuff which could sometimes taste like brown cardboard boxes but which seemed to be the perfect accompaniment to Celtic's Jim Brogan tackling like a car crusher or Partick Thistle's Denis McQuade being dispossessed by a half-time majorette left on the park, post-display, or St Johnstone's John Connolly gliding serenely over a glass-ily frozen penalty box in the manner of Raeburn's *Skating Minister*.

Pi is a mathematical constant. Pie is a football constant. At East Fife it's a Methil-matical constant. At Hamilton it's an Academical constant. Three million are consumed at Scottish grounds every season so in our football the pie – mutton, as grey as the gloweringest sky, accept no substitute – is just about as crucial and as non-nego-tiable as the ball. It's an irresistible force in the game but, on balance, I think I probably prefer Dunfermline Athletic's steak bridie, an immovable object once consumed, a depth charge to the gut, reas-suringly lodged in the same place for the duration of the match and a good bit beyond.

In England, football has changed out of all recognition and the menu with it. Manchester United's prawn-sandwich brigade marked the beginning of the middle-classisation of the game there and the end of atmosphere. Then Roger Nouveau Football Fan* and his berkish mates probably swapped sides when Manchester City opened the Tunnel Club, a £15,000-a-season 'immersive hospitality experi-ence' where rich rubberneckers could look down on the supporters in the cheap(er) seats and up at the superstars, tantalisingly close in the stadium's innards, then swap stories over posh nosh: 'Jack Greal-ish was wearing these really cool headphones and he completely blanked me!' ... 'Kevin De Bruyne was on his phone although I don't think he was actually talking to anyone!'

City, when they were at Maine Road, were salt of the earth; now at the Etihad they're 'salt cod croquette'. Roasters can dine on 'roast pork belly' while 'ox cheek bourguignon' and 'grilled Padrón peppers' are popular with the kind of supporters who might wear plum-coloured breeks to football completely unironically.

This stratification of fans, based on what they can spend to fill their fat faces, has yet to come to Scotland. Ibrox is still an immersive

* *The Fast Show*'s fake fan

hostility experience. 'Are you wantin' a Smax?' can be open to interpretation here. The pie remains at the top of our football food chain. Who's to say Mariah Carey, with that notorious pretend-nibble of Walkers crisps in her 2019 Christmas commercial, wasn't actually yearning for a Chipmunk? But even the snob chefs at the Tunnel Club bow down to those bold hucksters bearing boxes of treats by rounding off the great feast with a tribute to oor fitba's finest – 'macaron selection'.

And maybe, as the plum breeks threaten to burst asunder on the way out of the Etihad, one of the greedy gormandisers will be heard to confess: 'Don't know about you but I would have been happy with just a waspburger.'

32

'*Hunkering down in the long grass with*
The Observer Book of Birds? *That was pervy*'

ALEX MACDONALD, ORNITHOLOGIST, IS SURPRISED BY WILLIE WALLACE, A HORSEMAN RIDING BY

Now I like Frankie Boyle, he's a funny guy, but I reckon the comedian got it wrong when he called Kirkintilloch the worst wee town in Scotland. Had I, in this corner of East Dunbartonshire, not just enjoyed a cappuccino in an Italian bistro advertising a 'theatre menu', which would seem to indicate the existence nearby of a troupe of amateur thesps if not an actual proscenium arch? And was I not then dauner-ing along a pleasant waterway, all swollen and lush from the summer downpours?

Not just any old waterway either but the Forth–Clyde Canal and somewhere on its banks – almost Constable-esque – there occurred an event which grips me, giving lie to the idea that nothing remark-able ever happens in Kirky. It was an encounter between two guys from a more innocent age – before footballer downtime consisted of PlayStation, shopping for designer clobber in Harvey Nicks and, on free weekends, wingdings to Dubai. And I can't work out what's more remarkable: that Willie Wallace of Celtic was on horseback or that Rangers' Alex MacDonald was birdwatching.

Wallace, the Lisbon Lion, probably wouldn't be allowed to ride horses if he was playing now. Insurance would see to that. Maybe his manager, Jock Stein, disapproved but the Big Man had his work cut out making sure his charges weren't bevvying. His crack espionage unit needed to have eyes and ears on every pub within the fabled ten-mile radius of Parkhead; spies couldn't be dispatched round stables as well.

At least horse riding was Marlboro Man macho. Twitching on the other hand was a brave pursuit for a footballer. Racing pigeons was just about acceptable, if still slightly odd, but hunkering down in the long grass with *The Observer Book of Birds* and a flask of oxtail soup for hours at a time and studying our feathered friends? That was pervy. The yellow van would be round right away.

Sadly, there is no plaque marking the spot where Wispy met Doddie, so I had to duck inside Kirkintilloch Rangers Supporters' Club, stuffed with mementos of MacDonald's Euro triumph with the Gers, to learn about it. 'Every Wednesday, my day off, me and this old neighbour went spotting,' he explained. 'Actually, Auld Jock used to do rather more than that. He was into breeding different birds so he'd lay traps for them. This was illegal, of course, and even though I was just watching, I dare say I'd have been the one splashed across the front pages if we'd been found out.

'When the horseman happened by that day down at the canal, I did wonder if this was the mounted polis but it was just Willie. I didn't know he was into horses and there's no way he could have known I was into birds.

'I suppose it must have looked hilarious, the two of us going about our daft wee hobbies. If a supporter of Rangers or Celtic turned up, he wouldn't have believed it. I don't think Willie and I said very much to each other, maybe just a nod. It was like we'd met on the golf course or down the bookies, except we very definitely hadn't.'

Wallace, a Kirkintilloch native who's long been exiled in Australia, grew up a country boy. At the neighbouring farm the young lad milked cows and helped with the harvests. But MacDonald had a most urban childhood in the heart of industrial Glasgow in Tradeston, so why birds? 'Dunno,' he smiled, 'but I've always found them fascinating. We lived in Scotland Street where every Sunday night one of the local shops became this market where the enthusiasts would buy and swap birds. As a laddie I loved to listen to these guys' patter and even though we were in the city you could still see birds in the closes, disappearing into tiny holes in the walls. Up the railway line there were a lot of doocots and I knew just about everyone who had an aviary.'

If you remember MacDonald as a player – perpetual motion, pugnacious, a pest – it was funny to be sipping red wine with him on that Tuesday afternoon and chit-chatting about the quiet, slow charms of ornithology. Were STV, who now tailor separate broadcasts for the east and west coasts, to devolve its transmissions ever further and launch a strictly Kirkintilloch channel, he could be the nature correspondent. How about *Summerwatch*, not with Bill Oddie but Doddie?

'Birds make a rare hobby,' he continued. 'I don't do so much of it now because me and my wife Christine like to holiday in Spain so I can get some sun on my old, beat-up bones, but the grandkids are showing an interest so maybe I'll have to get my books out.'

Admittedly this was ornithology with a distinct Frankenstein element. 'Auld Jock, he was pretty crafty. He used to lure the birds down by laying out food on this sticky solution which was really for catching rats. That sounds cruel but he was ever so careful to clean the stuff off their feet using margarine. He was trying to breed the British birds – bullfinches, greenfinches and goldfinches, which are the most beautiful of all – with canaries in the hope of producing new and different colours and a good whistle. At one time I had 15 canaries of my own but no one at Rangers ever got to meet them. These guys were more interested in a different sort of bird.'

Wallace never reported MacDonald to the Royal Society for the Protection of Birds and Doddie never told Jock Stein to get a posse together to round up that varmint Wispy.

'I see Willie when he comes back to Kirky,' said MacDonald. 'The last time he gave me a big hug. Our secrets are still safe, aye.'

33

'Sticking it to them'

ENGLAND'S WORLD CUP TRIUMPH – MADE IN SCOTLAND

Milkmen, sweet-scented Avon ladies, brush sellers, encyclopedia hucksters and, in my mother's choice description, 'Holy Willie the God-botherer' – just some of the folk who don't call round any more. And here's another one missing from doorsteps: the man from the Pru.

In 1962, when Prudential Insurance were encouraging you to take out cover against the Cold War, invasions from Mars and the death watch beetle, Jimmy Greaves called Jimmy Leadbetter the man from the Pru. It wasn't the worst insult in the world but what was Greaves getting at? That Leadbetter seemed too old to be a footballer, too unathletic and too straight – and that he surely had a dreary job to match? But this was 1962, remember, not quite 1963, the epic year. The Beatles hadn't yet released their first LP. Men still looked like Philip Larkin.

Pre-Fab Four, few gave off a youthful air, though Leadbetter – balding, crinkly eyes and spindly legs earning him the nickname 'Sticks' – seemed older than most and certainly most footballers. He played in an indeterminate position for unfashionable Ipswich Town, a countrified team from the back of beyond, the kind who might have encouraged this chant from fans of city slickers like Greaves's

Tottenham Hotspur: 'Where's your straw, country yokel, where's your straw?'

But the yokels became the champs. Spurs, intent on successfully defending their old First Division title, were among many who woefully underestimated Ipswich, Leadbetter and the strange, strange way he played.

How he played was revolutionary. As revolutionary, considering the carefully ordered world of English football at the time, as Fadd9, the clanging guitar chord with which the Beatles would blast into 'A Hard Day's Night'. Before 1961–62, wingers hugged the touchline and full-backs always knew where to find them. Then along came Jimmy, on pins so scrawny that his shin pads met at the back, who'd sit deep, drift inside, dawdle, drift some more, and doubtless metropolitan football thought he was searching for a suitable stile where he could rest up and inspect the livestock, corn stalk protruding from his mouth.

He was given this freedom by his manager, Alf Ramsey, who four summers after the championship came to Suffolk, took his 'wingless wonders' wheeze into the international arena where England lifted the World Cup. You could say our Jim won it for them.

Edinburgh-born Leadbetter, after making the quantum leap from Armadale Thistle to Chelsea earlier in his career, was drifting at Portman Road, although not in a good way, when Ramsey turned up. With no bright lights in the town to attract much glamour, the manager had to work with the players he had, improvise and convert. And when he came up with the idea of a 'deep winger', Ramsey must have thought he'd invented sexual intercourse, inspiring Larkin into verse.

Leadbetter's role bamboozled opponents, the practitioner's demeanour provoking additional amusement and amazement. Pat Godbold, club secretary during 1961–62, told me: 'Some people wondered how Jimmy got in the team and they used to joke he was related to Alf. I guess one or two might have thought he was Alf's dad.'

Ray Wilson, then of Huddersfield Town, said: 'Jimmy had to be 60 at least.' Team-mate Ray Crawford said: 'When I clapped eyes on this knock-kneed fella I thought he was my granddad.' Roy Bailey, nervous on his first day at the club, nipped to the loos before meeting Ramsey: 'The cubicle door was being blocked by this ancient geezer sitting on the toilet, smoke billowing from him. I went to the manager's office: "Mr Ramsey, there's an old man in your toilets smoking a fag." Alf said: "The elderly chap of which you refer is one of my best players, Jimmy Leadbetter."'

This yarn chimed with one Godbold told about Ramsey, how in all the time working for him she didn't know he smoked until, passing his office and seeing him at his roll-top desk engulfed in a fug, she thought he was on fire and quickly raised the alarm. Out on the pitch, Ramsey and Leadbetter's smoke-and-mirrors subversion of the winger's duties was even more startling.

Wilson again: 'Ipswich that season looked like a team of journeymen and has-beens and then there was Jimmy. But he was magnificent. We had the right-back follow him everywhere and our man would end up stranded in their box, leaving 50 yards of space. They got away with that system for years.'

It seems ridiculous that they did but then these were simpler times. Now, every game is televised, every tactic and trick flagged up. The analysis department will have an exhaustively detailed DVD of the next opponents' last match on the manager's desk within an hour of it finishing. This was the age of endless football chatter away from the pitch, and hushed words behind hands and A3 notepads on the touchlines. Few clubs back then spied on Ipswich. There were no fast roads into Suffolk and the train line wasn't yet electrified. But arrogance contributed to the ignorance, along with complacency and much chortling over Leadbetter's physical appearance.

For Wilson and other full-backs, the feeling of disorientation when encountering Sticks couldn't have been worse if they'd been hypnotised, dressed up as a Tiller Girl, spun round a few times and woken with a snap of the fingers to find the crowd pointing and laughing at them. By then, Leadbetter, deploying what Crawford termed 'a lovely drag-back which always left the other team on their bottoms', had long since dispatched a cross from an angle that had defied the conventional geometry of football. Crawford or fellow striker Ted Phillips simply added the finishing touch.

Another victim of the spectral, string-and-bone Scot was Fulham's George Cohen. 'We were playing something I simply didn't recognise,' he said of Ipswich's system. 'I didn't know who the heck I should be marking.' By the time the World Cup came round, Cohen and Ray Wilson were the England full-backs. Added Crawford: 'In '66 Alan Ball was Jimmy. If Jimmy hadn't made such a success of Alf's system I don't think England would have won the World Cup.'

You might wonder what Alf and his 'dad' talked about during fag breaks, for it probably wasn't Scotland. Ramsey called Scots 'those strange little men'. When he brought England north of the border Hampden baited him. 'Welcome to Scotland,' offered a local pressman on one such visit, to which Ramsey replied: 'You must be fucking joking.' But a Scot was the prototype for his masterstroke.

Leadbetter didn't quite possess the 'ash hair, toad hands and prune face' of Larkin's 'The Old Fools'. Age-wise, he wasn't quite the Beatles' fabled 64. If he really did resemble the man from the Pru, tendering his policies for approval, then no one bothered to read the small print which enabled him to dauner so devastatingly. Ramsey's praise was, for the manager, pretty fulsome: 'Yes, he was Scottish, but I owe him so much.'

34

'A goal to have Space Race kids dreaming of exciting planets waiting to be explored'

WILLIE CARR'S DONKEY KICK

It was quite a moment in 1666 when an apple landed on Isaac Newton's head. Dropped right down, didn't meander. A no-nonsense plummet, a perpendicular plop.

But possibly more significant was the day in 1970 when a football travelled in the opposite direction.

Coventry City were playing Everton at Highfield Road, the home team winning a free-kick. The visitors formed a defensive wall and at that time four or five stout English yeomen willing to put heads of oak in the way would invariably do the trick and block the strike. No one in the domestic game could yet bend the ball round the human barrier, or get it up and over to score.

But a pint-sized patter merchant from Glasgow had an idea. Willie Carr stood over the ball and, gripping with his heels, flicked it up behind him. This perfect vertical ascent flummoxed the Everton yeomen, the fans in the ground and the television audience.

Then, having reached its highest point, the ball was beginning its routine Newtonesque journey to terra firma when the centre-forward Ernie Hunt stepped up and lashed it into the net for a phantasmagorical goal, a truly radical volley. It was the first goal screened in colour on the BBC's *Match of the Day* and so radical that previously all of TV, our sitting rooms, our lives, seemed to have existed in monochrome. The goal pranged a secret lever behind the net which turned the world dayglo. Suddenly we could see Coventry in sky blue, the bamboozled opposition in burnished yellow, tangerine trees and marmalade skies.

The donkey kick, as it was immediately christened, almost never happened. Carr and Hunt were one more botched effort away from ditching the routine altogether. 'We learned it off our coach, Bill Asprey, who'd been on a course at Lilleshall, but were getting nowhere,' Carr explained when I tracked him down to his greenhouse in the Shropshire village of Ackleton. 'Our attempts at training were hopeless. Either I wasn't flicking the ball properly or Ernie was hitting the corner flag with his volleys. The one time we tried it in a game, a pre-season friendly at Blackpool, he struck the stadium clock. It was strange the trick wasn't working because Ernie was a great volleyer but our team-mates were getting bored of it and frankly so were we.'

Carr when we spoke was waiting on a kidney transplant, having received this intimation of mortality shortly after Hunt's funeral in the summer of 2018. 'It was a bit of a shock. When you're a footballer, fit and running all over the place, you think you're going to live forever.' There's a chance, though, that his audacity and ingenuity will endure – as well it should.

A shot-blaster's son from Govan, Carr might never have ended up at Coventry if his mother hadn't run off with another man. In search of a fresh start and better luck, his father moved the family to England. Carr's big sister had gone on a recce to Cambridge and was followed by one of his brothers. 'They both found jobs easily and reported back: "It's different here." So Dad and the rest of us packed up all our stuff and jumped on a bus.' This was Carr's own personal dayglo moment, prior to the goal. 'We got off at a lovely little place called St Neots on the banks of the Ouse. There was a regatta, there was sunshine. I said to myself: "Oh my God, this is great!"'

Though schooled in the game in the south, Carr was very definitely a product of the renowned, gold standard Scottish assembly line which turned out tiny, twinkle-toed but tough practitioners of midfield cunning. Just about every English club had one and just about every big club in London fancied Carr but he chose Coventry, thinking he'd make the breakthrough earlier there. Plus, they had something different about them. 'I don't know what it was,' he said. A flair for innovation? 'Aye, maybe.'

Jimmy Hill was the manager-cum-impresario. 'We were a provincial, unglamorous club and Jimmy was always dreaming up schemes to boost our profile. He was larger than life and ahead of his time. He changed the strip to sky blue. We had our own train for the fans, the Sky Blue Express, with away days bingo.' For home games there was pre-kick-off and half-time razzmatazz, free juice and snacks for the kids and a classy match programme, more like a glossy magazine. And there was the donkey kick.

'Against Everton I think I popped the ball too high but in any case their wall stayed rooted because none of them knew what was going on,' continued Carr. 'I kind of walked away all nonchalant, didn't I? What a goal. I loved Ernie, loved his big grinning mug and his clowning around in training with gorilla masks and lassies' wigs, but I didn't think he was going to score that day!'

Neither did Barry Davies although the commentator gave the impression he did. There was a gasp, then the man at the mic exclaimed: 'And they don't come much better than that!' Was this an odd phrase? Did it suggest Davies had been caught out by the donkey kick like everyone else? Maybe he was trying to suggest he had insider knowledge from many training grounds and that the donkey kick had been a work in progress for every club, and a race to see who could perfect it first. There had been attempts, modifications, complete rejigs, countless hours expended in pursuit of the eureka moment. Well, here it was in glorious Technicolor, instigated by a Scotsman with hair the shade of Irn-Bru.

If there was any proprietorial intent from Bazza then it was lost on a generation of schoolboys. Back in playgrounds up and down the land the excitable cry was 'You be Willie and I'll be Ernie'. We were trying to replicate the most spectacular goal seen in football until that point. And when we succeeded, and plastic polka-dot balls scudded off toilet-block walls as the small, speccy goalies clutched at thin air, we rejoiced with Davies's words, which weren't lyrical or profound and might have been self-serving but what the heck: 'And they don't come much better than that!'

Now, you might think I'm exaggerating the goal. If you were too young or not even born when Carr and Hunt magicked it up and you're over-familiar with Cristiano Ronaldo's sleight of foot and all the tricks of today, maybe it doesn't look anything special. But context is everything. Although Pelé had dummied outrageously (vs Uruguay) and shot from halfway (Czechoslovakia) in the World Cup four months previously, even back-heels were rare in domestic football. Elsewhere, we were tremendously impressed by Meadowlark Lemon's finger spins with a basketball, by illusionist David Nixon's dematerialising rabbit, and by the muscleman on *Opportunity Knocks* making his heavily oiled torso talk. These were more innocent times, for sure, and it didn't take much to induce gasps. But a ball had never travelled like this before, straight up in the air. Even if it didn't travel far, it couldn't have made a more unerring rise if it had been tethered to a rocket launch pad. And even if it only hung motionless for a millisecond, this was enough to have the Space Race kids conjuring up images of tiny moons floating serenely in the solar system and beyond them exciting planets just waiting to be explored.

Carr and Hunt made a great double act and like all great ones they were different: Hunt the beefy, grinning Englishman; Carr much less demonstrative. But the Scot's stealth was highly effective and never more so than that day in 1970. And for the record, Pelé's fancy-dannery over in Mexico didn't actually result in goals being scored.

Carr won six caps, and a 1972 friendly against Peru was a collector's item for aficionados of a tartan archetype: 'The midfield was me, Archie Gemmill and Asa Hartford – surely the tottiest that's ever represented Scotland.' Then, after he'd finished playing, Carr was able to walk tall in sales. 'As a rep the donkey kick was my calling card. Meeting someone for the first time, it broke the ice. "Talk me through it," they'd always say.' And his employers? They manufactured ball bearings, so in a way Carr was able to continue his mystical work with spheres.

The donkey kick was attempted one more time that season, Hunt striking the bar with his effort against Tottenham Hotspur, and then it was banned. Said Carr: 'UEFA decided it wasn't legitimate because using both feet I'd touched the ball twice and by being flicked straight up in the air it hadn't travelled its full circumference. At the time I thought that was complete rubbish – football's entertainment, after all – but I suppose it's made the goal even more special.

'That daft trick has been good to me and I guess it's what I'll be remembered for. Cannae complain about that.'

35

'Seven oaters a year, all of them stoaters'

WILLIE DONACHIE'S READ
WAR AND PEACE. HAVE YOU?

One of my favourite features in *Mad* magazine was the 'Scenes We'd Like to See' comic strip where common convention was inverted by people you thought you knew, doing something surprising or even shocking.

For instance, tweedy intellectuals with terrifyingly big brains would be semi-comatose on burst sofas amid the detritus of an epic beer 'n' burger binge as the eggheads argued over who was the 'Playmate of the Month' they'd be most likely to give up philosophical theorising for.

Or – this never quite appeared in my favourite mag – Scotland footballers in the Hampden tunnel just before kick-off would be discussing literature.

Well, why not? Why couldn't Jimmy Johnstone and Willie Donachie be sharing opinions and recommendations on books they'd read in downtime? Because read them they did.

The chat between these two, team-mates in dark blue in 1972, might have gone like this:

Donachie: 'What have you got on the go just now, Jinky?'
Johnstone: 'Just the latest Edson.'

Donachie: 'Edson Arantes do Nascimento? When did Pelé move into fiction?'

Johnston: 'No, J.T. Edson, the cowboy chronicler. Never been to America, never even sat on a horse, but imagines the Wild West from a semi in Melton Mowbray. Great on the detail of gun jams and card scams. Bashes out seven oaters a year and they're aye stoaters. Hates the permissive society, trendy intellectuals and books with a "message" but loves corny jokes. The men are strong and silent; the women "fast-ridin', hard-lovin'"'. If J.T. doesn't like you – Labour politicians, trade union bosses – he'll stick you in a yarn and you'll have an unfortunate affliction or a messy end. No book will ever contain fewer than 12 good scraps. I'm halfway through *Gunsmoke Thunder* and there's already been eight. So, what about you, Willie, what are you reading?'

Donachie: '*Siddhartha* by Hermann Hesse. Set in Ancient India, 14 centuries before your guys were riddling each other with holes. How's this for corny? A J.T. reworking might be called *Sieve-hartha*. This is a counterculture classic, a hippy bible. Hesse's heroes maybe aren't a million miles from J.T.'s – sensitive, brooding, of independent mind and always searching for something. Timothy Leary advised: "Before your LSD session, read *Siddhartha*." But even on just macaroon bars it's making perfect sense to me.'

Johnstone: 'Nice one, Willie. Sounds like you prefer deeper meaning to mean critters. But you know, we dedicated readers should have minds as wide as the prairies and be receptive to new concepts such as the railroad. Let's swap books when we've finished them.'

Maybe my rubbish jokes do Donachie a disservice. He's just about the most soft-spoken, reflective, interesting character I've met in Scottish football. And he's definitely the best-read. As well as *Siddhartha* he's devoured *War and Peace*. All 587,287 of Leo Tolstoy's words. What's more, this was on the Manchester City team bus. 'The very fact I was reading a book amused the rest of the guys as they played cards,' he told me. 'And when they found out which one I'm sure they all would have thought I was weird.'

Not weird exactly but wondering, just like a Hesse hero. As a boy who lost his mum at 12, saw his poor dad take refuge in drink, was exposed to Glasgow's religious divide and needed to always be looking over his shoulder for the bovver boys, he had a few questions he needed answering.

'Oh, just the big ones,' Donachie smiled. 'What's life about? What are we here for? Where are we going?' He thought he was probably quite irritating on the gargantuan issues. 'I remember asking a priest who was also a science teacher how that was possible because I couldn't square the two disciplines.'

His soul-searching had taken him from the Gorbals to Gandhi, Manchester to meditation. The quest was a search for happiness and it was ongoing, confirmed by a quotation from *War and Peace*: 'Let the dead bury the dead, but while I'm alive, I must live and be happy.'

Donachie made lifelong friends in No Mean City and a trio of mates all now live on the far side of the world. Like them he had to get out and at 16 signed for Man City. Most young footballers of his generation pitching up in a new town might first have sought out a snooker hall; this one signed up for a course called Practical Philosophy.

He was into mindfulness before the term was coined. He investigated Buddhism and was turned on by Vedanta, the ancient Hindu philosophy believing in self-knowledge – 'The search for the God within' – and self-reliance. Practical Philosophy espouses 'self-enquiry' and 'self-discovery'. All of that, all of these 'selfs', amount to quite a lot of DIY. Footballers these days are assumed not to be able to tie their bootlaces without assistance from one of the coaching staff, even requiring help with something as simple as buying a desert island or a Maserati. Donachie was a bit bolder.

When he coached at Man City and the club were languishing in the third tier, a big player was Andy Morrison, the Kinlochbervie cult hero among Sky Blues who'd begun the last year of the century in a Highlands police cell after a brutal drinking session. Morrison was prone to suicidal urges before Donachie came to his aid. 'I took him along to Practical Philosophy and the lectures seemed to open his mind and he was able to find some peace.'

But meditation – how did that work in a footballing context? Presumably he kept that to himself. Actually, no. As manager of Millwall he was unafraid of suggesting to players having to uphold the ruffest, tuffest, toughest reputation in the land that they might give it a go pre-match. 'There was some resistance but pretty soon the guy who was most against it was shutting his eyes so he could still the mind before games.'

I never had the chance to ask Johnstone about J.T. Edson but know he was a fan because Bobby Lennox told me. 'We got into cowboy books at the same time,' said Jinky's fellow winger in the Lisbon Lions. 'They were uncomplicated – Leftie could always outgun Hank and Hank could always outgun Bronco – and so great for us first-time readers.

'They helped us relax before big games and in afternoons down at Seamill* the rest of the team would be enjoying a wee sleep while we'd be lost in our shoot-'em-ups. I've read everything Edson wrote. And you could always count on him for a terrific fight between two women.'

Now a fabulous image presents itself. Jinky is leaping off his bed, wondering on his dash down the hotel corridor if in the future there might be such things as book groups where readers meet up to enthuse over favourite novels. Then he raps on his team-mate's door: 'Bobby! Page 47! Tell me if that isn't Ol' J.T.'s best lassie-vs-lassie punch-up yet!'

* Celtic's R&R venue before big games.

36

'There is nothing like a Dane'

MORTON'S SCANDI INVASION

The most vivid memory I have from the very first Scottish game I attended is of the Hibernian centre-half soaring majestically for the ball against Clyde and then, immediately afterwards and equally majestically, a red geyser erupting from the top of his head. The player had his blond hair cropped short in a buzz-cut style popular among the GIs in my American comics so I had no difficulty seeing the blood spurt. It was gruesomely fascinating, like my favourite bubblegum card depicting more US conflict: Union soldiers on horseback being impaled on Confederate spikes in the Civil War. But this gore-spattered casualty wasn't American – John Madsen was Danish.

The year was 1967, I was ten, and didn't yet know of this country called Denmark. What I strongly suspected was that they bred 'em tough as Madsen was quickly back heading the ball, even though his bandage resembled a wonky turban – even though the blood kept coming, along with some cruel laughter from the terraces.

How exotic of Hibs to have a Danish stopper – but how exotic of Morton to have 11 Danes, an entire team, pass through their doors for the duration of a bold experiment. And how generous and come-all-ye as well, because while English football at that time didn't welcome foreign imports, the Scottish game did, and this was thanks in a large part to Haldane Y. Stewart.

You could call him Hal. You could call him Morton's manager but circus ringmaster/backstreet hustler/musical-hall illusionist/hilarious chancer would be more accurate. In 1964, Copenhagen club Brønshøj were invited to Greenock for a friendly. Their goalie played a stormer and Stewart, possessed of a soft hat but a quick mind, wanted to sign him. How much would he cost? Nothing, Danish football being amateur. 'That's my man!' rasped Stewart, like he'd just hit upon the idea for a great new variety act, which in a way he had.

Erik Sørensen took up the story: 'A Danish journalist told Hal there was an even better keeper at home – me. A lot of us Danes fancied trying pro football but there was a risk. You had to give up the international team and at that time Denmark were in the finals of the European Nations Cup. Go pro and there was a quarantine of two years before you could return to the team and maybe you wouldn't get back.

'So I got to hear about this British club interested in me and I thought: "How can this be?" "It's not England," I was told, "it's Scotland." "Oh ..."

'I flew to London and then on to ... where was it again? ... Abbotsinch. That was where I met Hal – what an awakening. First thing he said was: "Pretend to be a shipping agent who's come to work in Scotland." I had to do that to get through immigration control.

'Hal told me Morton had won all their games, that they'd just played Rangers in the final of the Scottish League Cup in front of 105,000 and that it was 0–0 at half-time.* Very soon, he said, they would be competing with Real Madrid. Hal was something special. His way of talking and dealing, ohmigod: like the ABC of salesmanship! Brilliant.

---

* In the second half Rangers banged in five goals.

'I maybe wasn't sure how he was going to find the money for this big dream but I really liked him. We chatted about my contract, he named a figure, and I made him put another zero on the end. "You're a good negotiator," he said. "Not as good as you," I said. Then I met the team – an hour before kick-off for a game against Third Lanark. Hal said: "I know, you're going to be Mr X for tonight." I told him that was OK and took my kit from my bag. Hal said: "You play in all black? That's brilliant!"'

Four years before Cadbury's utilised a dark-clad stranger to leap around daringly to promote Milk Tray chocolates, Stewart had Sørensen do this to flog Morton. The wheeze got the club on to the Old Firm-dominated back pages and got fans through the Cappielow turnstiles. Stewart asked the goalie: 'Any more like you at home?' There were. Sørensen: 'We soon had quite a few Danes whose names ended in "sen". Hal wanted them set out in the match programme together, a whole forward line of "sens". "But they're not all forwards," I said. "Disnae matter!"'

I met Sørensen, retired back to Denmark, when he returned to Greenock to look up old friends. Like many Scandinavians exposed to a distinctive and abrasive accent, traces of the tail o' the bank remain. 'My team-mates were great and helped me with the language. 'I'd say: "What's that word you use all the time, it seems to have so many meanings?" Hugh Strachan said: "What the fuck are you on about?" I said: "That's the one!"'

The sens included Jørn Sørensen (no relation), Kai Johansen, Carl Bertelsen and Madsen. Preben Arentoft was one of the next to arrive. Down the phone from Copenhagen he spoke in the same tones. Arentoft hadn't forgotten his first impressions of Greenock ('Cold, dark and stormy – I felt right at home') or his first glimpse of Scottish football ('It was Rangers vs Hibs, ohmigod, a lot of accidents, really rough, the centre-forward nearly killed the centre-half').

Despite the fierceness of the weather and the football – despite pan-global high street homogeneity being some way off, enabling towns in foreign lands to stay individual and strange – the Danes survived. Possessed of sensible haircuts and chunky thighs, they were good travellers and good competitors. Arentoft again: 'We learned the golf and how to lose money at cards. Glasgow was nice to visit and Edinburgh, too, for the castle and the famous street down below. The Scottish food? Well, we liked the battered fish.' Another of Morton's Danes, Børge Thorup, added: 'I'd never eaten a pie with the grey meat before but you know, I still love them today.' Thorup sounds like he achieved second-stage integration and indeed he's settled in Scotland and lives across the Clyde estuary in Dunoon.

'We got on well together, the Danes and the Scots, although there was a moment when we thought we might be for home,' said Arentoft. 'The Scots called a meeting, the union man was there, and someone said: "Raise your hand if you don't want any more Danes." I said, "Who's going to score your goals, then?" and everyone laughed. The protest was a joke – at least I think it was. Then Per Bartram and Bjarne Jensen came and they brought a load more goals.'

Half a century after Børge there would be a UK-wide obsession with *Borgen*. The Scandi-noir TV shows and the cosy lifestyle known as hygge were never out of the Sunday supplements. But the sens supplementing Saturdays at Cappielow did Greenock just fine. 'Morton's crowds grew to 10,000 when we were there; I think the fans liked us,' said Thorup. Sørensen agreed, adding: 'Maybe only once or two times did I hear a shout of "Ach, go home, ya bam!"'

I asked the Danes for a memory of Hal Stewart. Sørensen: 'Cup of tea and a wee roll, watching us train.' Thorup: 'He was, how you say, a ducker who was also a diver but a funny man too. "Keep the ball up in the air," was his favourite advice, "that way the opposition cannae get it."' Arentoft: 'He was awfie slow to pay us. I can still see him, pulling the lining from the pockets of his trousers, jacket and coat: "Sorry, boys ..."'

But as he wheeled and dealed and tried to keep Morton relevant if not quite Real, Stewart allowed some of his Scandi stars to move to bigger clubs: Sørensen and Johansen to Rangers, Thorup and Bartram to Crystal Palace, Madsen to Hibs and Arentoft to Newcastle

United whom he helped win the Inter-Cities Fairs Cup: 'The Scots didn't have any problem saying my name but the Geordies did so they called me Benny.'

So Morton got to be sophisticatedly continental and the Danes got to eat pies. It sounds like Scotland enjoyed the better of this arrangement, but did we? Arentoft again: 'The thing I remember best about my time at Morton is the 8th of August 1966 because that was when I met my wife Jane.' Sørensen and Jensen married Gourock girls, Sandra and Julia, and in Dunoon, Thorup runs a guest house with his wife Donna, and when we spoke they'd just celebrated their golden wedding anniversary.

Honestly, those Danes. They come over here, they impersonate our shipping clerks, they adopt our sweary words, they score our goals – and they steal our women.

37

'Like being told I had a nice wee car or a nice wee penis'

PROGRAMME COLLECTING

I am standing in the gloom of a tiny shop where the lights can never be full beam or they'll ruin everything. On the walls, all the way up to the ceiling in plastic sleeves, there's a great, yawning tableau of club crests, cartoon figures with chunky calves, aerial views of stadia and side elevations where the grounds unapologetically resemble Albanian prisons.

There are lots and lots of action shots, some striking frostquake ones with orange balls, some with jam-packed terracings as a backdrop and the most popular, a goal captured from behind the net, through the criss-cross, with the keeper clawing at the hurtling sphere in vain – though apparently the only still image we want from football these days is of the scorer in the middle of a celebration pile-on, almost orgasming from all the acclaim.

My name is Aidan Smith and I'm a programme collector.

It used to be 'fanatic' and before that 'dangerous obsessive who might break into your house for one from Third Lanark's last-ever season', but I think I've got it under control now. Though I visit less often, I still know everyone in the shop – know their 'wants' and how long they've been waiting for the last, desperate, few pamphlets they need, for other enthusiasts to give up or die off.

There is no point in me starting up a conversation with them; I've tried before and got nowhere. These guys – no women, at all, ever – are only here for their own holy grails which, once admitted, tend not to get mentioned again. It's as if the collectors are missing a body part, a highly embarrassing deficiency, rather than there simply being gaps in the leatherette binders back at home.

They don't do general chit-chat either and never seem to have an opinion about football's latest rumpus or to have watched the previous night's game on TV. I'm convinced some don't actually like the sport; indeed one admitted he travelled all the way to Ayr United, made the necessary purchase outside the stadium then left without seeing the game. Others told tales of panic and paranoia, of sprinting right round grounds trying to find vendors as kick-off neared and at other times of holding one's breath that the stewards were being truthful: programmes would be on sale inside. What Sad Sacks, I said to myself, before remembering that I could have been one, too.

Splashing £@!# on a Hajduk Split programme, written in Serbo-Croat, obviously. Blowing another chunk of the kids' inheritance on a record of the day my team scored ten at Partick Thistle. Inventing a secret code for the notebook so my wife wouldn't know how much I'd spent on the one from an 11–1 triumph at Airdrieonians. This was me when I was having programme-themed nightmares about my street turned into a raging river and leaving the family to perch, terrified, on the roof of a bus shelter while I frantically swam after the team sheet from a Blackpool friendly, the special issue for a pre-season tournament at Inverness Thistle and the official record of that first-ever game, Hibs vs Clyde in 1967.

The shop is smelly on account of all the ancient paper that's passed through Bovril-spattered hands and been stored in foosty attics before it ended up on these walls where rarity and covetability have determined that the programmes must sell for up to 10,000 times the original cover price. In 1967 it was three old pennies. 'Go on,' said my father, handing me the cash and pointing towards the bunneted seller with his drooping fag. My very first financial trans-action.

But I don't mind the pong or the silence because I love programmes. There is nothing else in my possession which can, instantly and vividly, remind me not just of the vanquishing of the mighty Bully Wee but of Dad and the John Lennon cap he always wore to the football. The snuff he spooned on to the back of his hand for the ritualistic half-time snort. The trepidation at being left at the terracing wall which was the best vantage point for one so small while he went to stand – these were carefully counted – 12 steps further back. And all of the fear disappearing as soon as I was befriended by a gaggle of gamine, mini-skirted teenyboppers who swooned and screamed at the young right-wing sensation whenever he hurtled down our side of the park, Beatles moptop bobbing. Just the one programme can do all of that.

As well as the nostalgist in me, programmes appeal to the anorak, also the completist and the fantasist. Hitting an impasse, for instance when large-form Dundee United ones proved elusive, I couldn't walk by a tenement block without imagining that the top floor housed a small and ancient collection, returned from games crease-free under gabardine raincoats, stored between sheets of sturdy brown paper and, for good measure, turned through a mangle once a year.

My ambition was to own all Hibs' homes and aways for the 1960s and 1970s. I already had many of the programmes from having been at the games although – embarrassed by my primary school scrawl and failure to spell Billy McNeill and Tommy Gemmell's names correctly when they'd scored goals, despite them being printed on the centre pages – I'd decided that pristine replacements were required. David Beckham's OCD had long amused me but now I appreciated what drove him to chill his cans of Coke with the labels facing the front. Presumably he makes sure the spines are showing on his first editions of the great philosophers as well.

If the shop didn't have what I needed, I went on eBay. What a garden of delight: the thrill of the countdown clock, leaving it until

0.07 secs to bid (never less than that, too dangerous), the smug joy of winning by 10p – and, crikey, the tension when I was in a duel with a 'private bidder' who had techniques and tricks of the long-term user at his disposal, and the near inevitability of being knifed in the tummy right at the death.

Being in the shop, mooching around, standing in solemn contemplation, pretending to study the walls even though we could all close our eyes and list most of what was on them, and their exact positioning, was like a game of poker, or indeed some interrogation room mind torture. No one was buying because there was rarely ever new stock. We were all waiting for a private audience with the boss for a chat about programmes and life – okay, just programmes.

If nobody left, then one of the guys might crack and feel obliged to say something. I thought I was being paid a compliment when a regular suddenly piped up: 'That's a nice wee collection you've got there.' Only later did it dawn on me that this was like being told I had a nice wee car or a nice wee penis.

I was small-time. The others were collecting every single programme bearing their team's name. That meant going right back to the 1930s, a realm of relentless torment, rusting staples, crumbling parchment and even more crippling prices. Little wonder the proprietor of our emporium was required to act as therapist and, occasionally, marriage counsellor.

For some, every single programme meant postponements, including matches called off late, the sellers having been allocated their bundles and unaware the documents in their mitts had just been confirmed as obscurely, perversely sacred.

Then there were the 'ghost games' which had been mothballed earlier in the week, only for a mystical, mythical handful of programmes – 'printers' copies' – to have been sneaked out. 'Hibs vs Motherwell, 1970, for instance,' explained the sad-eyed fellow for whom this was the bright elusive butterfly of love, the last to secure. 'I've never seen it; there were only two run off.' This for him, then, would be the equivalent of the British Guiana 1c Magenta from 1856, dubbed the *Mona Lisa* of the stamp world and believed to be the most valuable man-made item of any sort. Not for me, though. So long, losers!

I still need eight to complete. If I get them, fine. If I don't, that's the way it crumbles, cookie-wise, which is an old Billy Wilder line, and, hey, proof that there's a whole lot more than programmes going on in my life. But, you know, I'm thinking of starting up this subsidiary collection, just a small diversion to keep myself ticking over: notable Rangers defeats. I would need Berwick Rangers, obviously, and Chesterfield and Dunfermline Athletic ruining Christmas Day, 1965, for them and wee Arbroath shocking Ibrox. Raith Rovers shocking Ibrox and Rangers quickly signing Jim Baxter. St Johnstone shocking Ibrox and Rangers quickly signing hat-trick man Alex Ferguson. Oh, and of course Fergie as a Ger picking his nose when he should have been marking Billy McNeill in Celtic's 4–0 Scottish Cup final romp.

Brian, Norrie, David, I once was lost but now I'm found – great to see you guys again ...

38

'Obsession by Calvin Klein,
lager by Tennent's'

BRECHIN CITY'S HEDGE

Before me is a hedge. Not just any old common-or-garden hedge but the most famous hedge in world football. Correction: the only hedge in world football.

Brechin City's topiary, running down one side of the pitch, is, when fully sprouted, so verdant and lustrous that while Arbroath and Montrose centre-backs in Angus derbies can puncture it with a clearance resembling the ball being fired from a sail-powered warship's liveliest cannon, creating a perfectly round hole, mere mortals would of course want to stroke the hedge because, well, it's so beautiful.

And then a short while later you might wonder: can I gouge an opening big enough to crawl through – and what might I find on the other side?

Might I end up in AD 1000 … or 1988?

You see, both years are momentous in the town's history. In the countdown to tumultuous, terror-stricken AD 1000, when medieval Europe was gripped by panic that the new century would never arrive and the world would end, churches were crammed with repenters and ministers did a roaring trade offering comfort in return for property and gold. Not in

Brechin, though. Here they kept calm and built a tower.*

Eighty-six feet high. Round, like the ones in Ireland, good for bell-ringing, stashing significant trinkets and hiding out. While some of the Irish columns have detumesced to stumps, this one stands ever-phallic today, having predated the cathedral jammed up alongside which enabled Brechin to call itself a city, which in turn begat Brechin City their name, which in turn after many years of modest achievement begat the nickname 'Brechin City nil'.

Or would I, ducking out of the football, not seeing a goal coming from anywhere, burrow through the hole and end up in … Flicks! The Mearns' answer to Studio 54, this was Scotland's best night out – the post-disco boom, pre-rave explosion zenith of a richt guid time, and the furthest you could get from London smugness and posing. A hellzapoppin' experience set to 120bpm, it featured lasers, lads in suits, girls in not very much, Page 3 top-heavy titaness Samantha Fox, 'wacky, hilarious' Steve Wright from Radio 1 and *The Hitman and Her*, the wee-small-hours TV show which piped clubbing action into living rooms. The world didn't end in 1988 but that was the year the first acid house record crashed into the mainstream and the definitive YouTube clip of 'Stakker Humanoid' comes from Flicks, a kilted Pete Waterman championing the choon alongside Michaela Strachan as the royal burgh dances itself dizzy under a miasma of sweat, Obsession by Calvin Klein and lager by Tennent's.

And when I sneaked back through the hole into Glebe Park, what would I have missed? Maybe not much. Maybe it would indeed be 'Brechin City nil', except not on this day. The club were emerging from their first winter in the Highland League, having tumbled out of the SPFL. The hedge had yet to turn back from dull copper to vibrant green but on a sparkling March afternoon the team were banging in the goals, five of them against Nairn County.

I probably expected the players, the fans – and the hedge – to be

---

* The exact date of the tower's completion is lost in the mists of time but let's call it nice-and-neat AD 1000.

reduced by demotion. Nothing like. A banner on the tiny, roofed terracing behind the cemetery end read 'We fall together'. But full unfurling revealed the addendum: 'We rise together'.

There was no crush, and plenty of room for everyone, but I soon realised that right on halfway, hedge behind us, I was standing in a regular's favourite spot. Michael Forbes, 78, saw his first Brechin game from here in 1949. 'It was three old pennies for my dad and aged five I got in free,' he said, adding that when he was older he and his friends would sneak through a hole in the hedge. 'Now I've probably been coming the longest of anyone here, just beating an old boy in the main stand by a couple of years. He'll be over there in his bunnet. It's like we're in a Wild West fast draw against each other, except it's a gey slow one!'

Forbes was soon joined by his friends, a cheery bunch of mostly pensioners eager to hear the tales of the wild frontier from a couple of their number who ventured up to Buckie, a 'blingy' place where the fans like to lord it. For the Brechin players, the Highland was increasing the season's travelling by 2,000 miles. But after many years in the doldrums the fans were enjoying goals and victories. The 'pyramid' system has so far been aptly named for long-time senior teams who've fallen through the trapdoor; East Stirlingshire and Berwick Rangers seem entombed in their lesser division. Brechin, though, are hoping for regrowth, to bud again.

The hedge's splendour and specialness have only increased as stadia have become uniform. Previously, lots of grounds had their quirks and kinks and Archibald Leitch stands and suburban semi-detached pavilions among the features they could call their own. Then they lost their USP and became more B&Q. More flat-packy, more breeze-blocky, more like each other. Thus the hedge became more cherished. At the same time, football started to tap into the humour and eccentricities of the game in fanzines and on TV. The result was yet more kudos for the hedge and while it merely follows the far touchline at Brechin, never deviating, the impression given is that Louis XIV appointed Edward Scissorhands as head gardener and something crazy and mazey resulted, standing as the most elaborate privet imaginable.

A few years ago, the hedge was under threat from Euro regulations. UEFA decreed that the Brechin pitch would need to be widened by three metres to qualify for one of their licences. This was – there's no other word – hegemony, an attempt to force clubs into standardisation. Pre-Brexit, dull uniformity was the great Euro fear but I'd have cheerfully accepted non-curvy bananas, weaker vacuum cleaners and less buxom barmaids* as long as the hedge would stay exactly where it's always been. In any event, that threat disappeared.

'And hedges leafing with the green springtide,' wrote the poet John Clare, 'from out their greenery the old birds fly, and chirp and whistle in the morning sun; the pilewort glitters 'neath the pale blue sky, the little robin has its nest begun ...' Now, beware over-floweriness. Clare was a romantic poet and also one who, of his own volition, checked into the madhouse. In addition, pilewort being a treatment for haemorrhoids – not to be confused with 'Stakker Humanoid' – rather dulls the passion. And what is the purpose of Brechin's hedge but to merely act as a fence? That and to provide individuality. And identity. And indomitability, not least when the team went the entire 2017–18 season without winning a single league game then topping or bottoming that three years later with banishment from the senior game. The hedge is all of these things and more now that Flicks has shut its doors for ever. Michaela Strachan presents nature programmes these days. She should get herself back to Brechin with a camera crew and tell its wonderful story.

---

* Barmaids' half-measures and those other 'threats to civilisation as we knew it' were scare stories invented to rouse libertarians, Empire nostalgists and borderline racists to pull up their drawbridges and ultimately vote 'Leave'.

39

'Always laid-back, always "unroughled"'

THE FIRST SLEEPER-KEEPER

After that famous game between Brazil and Scotland in Seville at the 1982 World Cup, Socrates said two things that were at least the equal of his philosopher namesake's 'The unexamined life is not worth living'.

The first concerned David Narey's 'toe-poke', Jimmy Hill's description of our opening goal which some viewed as an insult tantamount to a challenge to war. Twenty-two years later, in of all places a primary school playground in Portobello, Edinburgh, the most steeple-esque midfield maestro there's ever been stooped low to exclusively whisper in my ear that the technique is much revered in Brazil and even has its own name: 'To hit with the toe, for disguise and surprise, is a classic play. This is bico.'

And do you remember what happened when, in response, Brazil won a free-kick just outside our box? Zico fired a ground-to-air missile which scudded the junction of crossbar and post* with the Scotland goalkeeper Alan Rough rooted to his line. The ball rebounded out to Socrates whose aim for the same corner looked to be deadly only

---

* In fact, Zico scored with his free-kick. Of course he did.

for Rough to somehow fingertip the ball away. Socrates rushed up to our man and gushed: 'Incrivel! [Incredible!] That is the best save I've ever seen! Surely one of the greatest of all time!' Whereupon Rough said: 'What the hell are you talking about, man? That was me trying to stop the first shot!'

Okay, the toe-poke stuff is perfectly true, but that's a Rough gag of the kind often told, and frequently by the 53-cap keeper against himself. Among the butter-fingered, the woodwork-colliding and the net-entangled, to say nothing of the bandy-legged and nutmeg-inviting, 'Scruff' might nestle third behind Frank Haffey and Stewart Kennedy as our most comical custodian – but is this entirely fair?

Yes, he lacked the immaculate bearing of Socrates and was the proverbial half-shut knife. Yes, he was the original sleeper-keeper. No, he didn't appear to have heeded the advice of the other Socrates who said: 'No man has the right to be an amateur in the matter of physical training. It is a shame ... to grow old without seeing the beauty and strength of which his body is capable.' And the Partick Thistle No. 1's favourite piece of terracing abuse during one of his dreamier, dwamier afternoons at Firhill was: 'Hey, Alan Rough, you'd better warm up because you're comin' aff.' But, you know, appearances can be deceptive.

Either blow-dried like the girls in the Harmony commercials* or bubble-permed, he kept goal for his country for a decade and at three World Cups. In Argentina in 1978 commentator David Coleman may have described him as 'inelastic' over his failure to stop strikes by Peru's Teofilo Cubillas but he'd been – cue the Detroit Spinners – the rubber-band man to greatly help Scotland to those finals, bending backwards to deny Wales's John Toshack for a career-best save.

---

* The ads featured attractive, young and usually blonde women out for a lunchtime stroll or a parkland jog back in the 1970s when lecherous men stalked the earth. Everything about the women bounced including their lustrous locks, and the oglers were dumbfounded to learn, as the pay-off had it: 'That girl's wearing Harmony hairspray!'

Was it Rough who attempted the splits in a Scotland–England match, creating enough space for a Clyde sewage boat, never mind a Kenny Dalglish trundler, as featured in so many bloopers tapes? No, that was his opposite number, the far more celebrated Ray Clemence, up Hampden's other end. Rough was a three-time victor over the Auld Enemy, twice at Wembley. And he did it all with a supremely nonchalant air, one-handed saves a speciality, which might have invited the odd, but erroneous, suspicion that he didn't care overmuch.

Don't worry, be Roughie. That was him, always laid-back, always 'unroughled'. 'I never had a sleepless night after a rotten game,' he said. 'Just before my Thistle debut, aged 16, Jackie Husband told me that there was no point being a goalie if I was a panic merchant. I heeded that.'

His first time at Wembley was after Kennedy had conceded five there. 'So, Alan,' he was asked by the BBC's Bob Wilson, 'is this going to be another Scottish disaster?' Surprised by the provocative nature of the enquiry, and from an ex-Scotland keeper as well, he perused the team sheet listing 'Rough, Partick Thistle' next to all the great glamour and smiled. The previous Saturday only 2,100 witnessed him stretch out his left arm to frustrate Dumbarton. Just before facing 100,000 he patted that arm, the one doctors wanted to amputate after a gang-hut accident as a kid.

Rough gravitated to the role in classic, cock-or-hen fashion – because he was useless outfield. 'When teams were picked in the playground or the park I'd be chosen after the boy in National Health specs, after the wee fatty, after the squirt trying to hide behind the wee fatty. Last one always went in goals.' Nowadays there must be university degree courses in goalkeeping, and specialist therapy for calamitous performances. He smiles at the fact England now travel to tournaments with no fewer than three goalkeeper coaches. In Argentina he didn't even have gloves, the only keeper there without a pair.

'So I think goalies have to be ... is insular the right word? You need to be mentally strong. But I don't know about mad. I've never thought of myself as especially eccentric.'

Hang on, though, wasn't he majorly superstitious? 'Ah well, you see, I got into the habit of not shaving before games. And I always had to hang my clothes on the 13th peg. I'd bounce a ball off the dressing-room wall a certain number of times – I forget how many – being careful not to stand on the unlucky bit of the floor. I wore a favourite old shirt under my top and always my own white socks, and continued to take them on Scotland trips even after the SFA got fussy about the team all wearing red ones. Away to Israel once I forgot to wash the socks from the last Thistle match so they were soaking wet from the sink and there was me, squelching around, soapy bubbles popping from the eyelets of my boots, but playing one of my best games for my country. After that I should have done it every time.'

Then, following the pre-game rituals there were the during-the-match ones. 'I used to have a hatful of lucky charms to stick behind the net. There was a scabby tennis ball, a thistle key ring, a couple of marbles, lots of daft wee trinkets – and when fans chucked more I'd have to put them in the bunnet, too. I liked to blow my nose a lot during games, and was always turning round to ask someone the time. And I had to have seven pieces of Wrigley's with me: three for each half and another for the last five minutes when things got exciting. So, yes, fairly superstitious.'

But not, he repeats, a worrier. 'I loved playing for Thistle and maybe I stayed there too long but that was me. I did eventually move to Hibs and remember Paul Kane asking me what I was going to do when I finished up playing. I was 33, he was 17, and I did wonder: "Maybe he's got a point ..."'

Perhaps his life was 'unexamined' but it was definitely worth living. 'I never thought about "career" or bothered about money,' he continued. 'All of my business ventures – the pub in Maryhill, the sports shop in Musselburgh – failed. But I absolutely loved standing in the tunnel at Wembley next to English superstars like Kevin Keegan and Emlyn Hughes when I was on just 40 quid a week and Scotland were about to walk on to the park and enjoy a memorable victory.'

Should we play out his story with another joke? A block of flats is on fire and up on the third floor a mother holding a small child is yelling for help. From the street below comes a hero's instruction: 'Drop the kid and I'll save him. I'm Alan Rough, Scotland's goalkeeper.' The woman, seeming to be even more panic-stricken now, shouts: 'Is there anyone else down there?'

40

'The curious incident of the dog just after half-time'

TED MACDOUGALL vs CHIC BRODIE: CLASH OF THE TITANS

Every time one Scot meets another on England's green and pleasant football fields, my little heart skips a beat and my chest swells to full sparrow dimensions. In these encounters my countrymen can be shaking hands or merely punching each other, it's all the same.

Dave Mackay throttling Billy Bremner with comic-strip kerpow-like intensity is what gets called iconic and with very good reason. These were giant characters and the conflagration happened at Wembley in a showpiece match, the Charity Shield. Capturing for posterity was ace photographer Monte Fresco.

But consider the shared moment, sadly not snapped, between Inverness-born Ted MacDougall and Chic Brodie, a son of Duntocher in West Dunbartonshire. This came immediately after the final whistle in an FA Cup tie on 20 November 1971. Chic was non-league Margate's goalie and Bournemouth's Ted had just banged nine goals past him. Brodie possibly wasn't iconic but he was certainly indomitable.

Walking off together, Brodie told MacDougall that the final score, 11–0, confirmed him as the world's most tragic keeper. Perfectly reasonably he might have retired the gloves there and then but he continued playing for another four years. Further mishaps are not recorded but he can't have been too far away from them.

There were plenty previously. Chic recalled the earlier ones for Ted including how, in 1964, for Brentford at Carlisle United, he was struck on the knee by a rock thrown from the crowd and had to be carried off. The following year he was down at Millwall. The denizens of the Den can get jittery if their hard-won reputation as football's biggest mentalists is threatened and they answered the rock with a grenade which was deposited in Brodie's cap. He always left the head-gear in the back of the net in case of bright and blinding sunshine. Fortunately the grenade turned out to be a replica. Then in 1970 against Lincoln City he was poleaxed by a fractured crossbar.

But worse was to come. Bizarro was to come. Away to Colchester United, a Jack Russell bounded on to the park. The ball was booted long and, showing terrific box-to-box energy, the dog gave chase, out-scampering everyone in the home team's attack. Brodie stepped forward for a routine retrieval only for the mutt to crash into him. He crumpled to the ground, the laughter of the crowd only slightly abating when a stretcher was requested.

Now, at first club Manchester City Brodie had been mentored by Bert Trautmann who famously didn't let a broken neck stop him from keeping goal in the 1956 FA Cup final. Brodie had been felled by a tiny pooch, it's true, but his kneecap was shattered. 'Aye the dog was a wee thing,' he reflected later. 'Bloody solid, though.'

The injury ended his career at senior level but he promptly went non-league with Margate, the kind of little dreamers who'll ring the dates on the calendar when the FA Cup holds out the prospect of glamour, a big windfall, a fairy-tale triumph, perhaps all three. And on very nearly the first anniversary of the curious incident of the dog just after half-time, Brodie headed along the south coast to Bournemouth.

MacDougall had always been a goal glutton, right from kids' football in the Highlands. In Widnes, Lancashire, as a junior compositor at the local newspaper he sneakily enlarged the headlines if he'd scored for his amateur team, which he usually had. In later years he would notice that goalscorers rarely declared themselves as such, fearful of recriminations if the strikes didn't come. He never suffered from coyness or self-doubt.

Bournemouth wanted some of that monomania, a man who would barge small children out of the way of a low cross delivered at an inviting pace into the six-yard box, but only secured his signature from York City after agreeing to throw in a set of curtains. MacDougall insisted: 'And you'd best make them velvet.'

Nicknamed Supermac, he approached the Margate tie as an opportunity to seriously boost his goal tally with the aim of beating the previous season's total of 49. He had specialist knowledge of the Dean Court ground and how to score there. In a seaside resort full of funfairs and their seductive stalls, this was his rifle range. He was like the shifty Scots proprietor who kept the only good shooter for himself, the rest having had their sights purposely knocked off line. On 20 November in walked the hapless Brodie who got strafed.

MacDougall extended sympathy to his fellow Scot after the hammering – 'Especially when he told me about the grenade, the daft dog and all the rest.' Nevertheless he was disappointed only to have scored nine, reasoning: 'I should definitely have got a couple more.' That would have beaten Joe Payne's ten for Luton Town back in 1936, the English record.

By his own admission MacDougall had become 'a right greedy sod'. Team-mates had long given up hope that he might pass to them. 'What's an assist?' he asked. 'Is that not something you go to the doctor to have lanced?' As it was, the nine gave him the best-ever haul in the cup, an achievement which still stands, and to the tune of TV's *The Banana Splits*, the Bournemouth fans sang: 'One MacDougall, two MacDougall, three MacDougall four, five MacDougall scores the goals and so do many more.' The feat turned him into a minor celebrity and the next day brought a phone call from Geoff Hurst: 'Could I play for a World XI in his testimonial? "Who else is coming?" I asked. "Oh, Eusebio, Uwe Seeler, Jimmy Greaves, Jimmy Johnstone, Dave Mackay, just those guys." So I bumped my little knackered car up to London to meet my team-mates in the Hilton, Park Lane. I was the only guy I'd never heard of.'

After football MacDougall moved to America and, improbably, became something of a fashionista, working for his French-Canadian designer wife. 'I always say I don't know what happened to football in the 1980s because I was in ladies' clothes,' he laughed. 'Lyne hired me twice and fired me twice. It was quite difficult going from football, which is obviously fairly macho, to fashion, a bit more camp let me tell you. I was tough with the girls and there were lots of tears. Lyne told me to be nicer and I did try: "Great shoes! I love your hair!" But I couldn't help wondering what Bill Shankly, my first boss, would have thought of me.'

Brodie was back between the sticks for Margate the week after Supermac's bonanza, no mental health support required. The next season his team pulled out an FA Cup plum, being drawn against holders Tottenham Hotspur. A record crowd at their ground saw him keep the defeat to an almost respectable 6–0. He died of cancer in 2000 but not before acquiring his own Geoff Hurst anecdote. His encounter with the England World Cup hero wasn't quite as glitzy as MacDougall's, though, because in his post-football life as a taxi driver he managed to collide with Hurst's Jaguar.

Poor Chic, the calamitous custodian right to the end.

41

'Wallace and Vomit'

RANGERS ON THE SAND DUNES

How do you know if someone's a wild swimmer? They'll tell you about it, usually within seconds of a conversation beginning, even if it's on a completely unrelated subject.

And in Gullane, East Lothian, on New Year's Day, 2022, there are plenty of them around. Wearing £200 dryrobes and little dimpled smirks of self-congratulation, they set up base camp for the great mission, carefully checklisting their kit for … what? Distress flares? Vials of cyanide? Farewell letters to loved ones? This is the warmest New Year's Day for a century, but you would think that no one has ever swum here before. You would think that these exhibitionists are the first to participate in any kind of physical exertion on this beach.

And yet … flashback to some long-lost summers. Gasping for breath on hands and knees, meaningful progress utterly beyond them, successive squads of Scottish footballers probably reckoned they were about to be swallowed up by the relentless sands, like airline passengers who'd staggered away from a crash in a desert, or lost Foreign Legion defectors.

Then, up ahead, something shimmered.

'Guys, guys … look! Have a fuckin' gander. What a beautiful sight fir sair eyes. We're gonnae be all right. We're gonnae be saved!'

What was this mirage, or who? Ursula Andress offering fresh water from her conch shells, perhaps, or Bo Derek tantalising with beer? Or maybe Yasmine Bleeth, prancing angel of mercy in a high-on-the-thigh scarlet maillot with her inflatables prominent, the favourite *Baywatch* kiss-of-life practitioner of *Friends'* Chandler and Joey for a much-loved scene chillin' on their La-Z-Boys: 'Run, Yasmine, run like the wind!'

Different generations, different optical illusions. But the same delirium and the same torture. This was pre-season training in Gullane, before the advent of sports science and the Health & Safety-esque directive that footballers cannot be (mal)treated like this. Although for some poor schmucks the hell of Murder Hill would continue.

Hearts were the first club to send their men over the dunes in the late 1960s and then the Rangers team of the following decade made Gullane notorious. Andress in the Bond movie *Dr. No* was probably the No. 1 beach goddess for these guys though it wasn't her they glimpsed through stinging eyes. Nor was it their era's worst nightmare in a sand-based setting up until that moment – Ian Hendry as that brutal bastard of a staff sergeant in prison movie *The Hill*. It was their manager, Jock Wallace.

Every time Wallace spoke – gravelly growl, jaw jutting – about yet another victory on the way to two domestic Trebles in three seasons, he explained the success in one word – 'character'.

The boss acquired his from being a commando, jungle fighting in Malaya and Northern Ireland postings during the Troubles. As a young coach at Hearts he'd witnessed the attempted ascents of Gullane's shifting sands and approved, so he pinched Murder Hill for his new detail.

Rangers stalwart Alex Miller had never seen anything like it: 'My first manager was Scot Symon and you might wonder how we ever won anything. First day back at training after the summer it was: walk a lap of Ibrox, jog, four sets of each, finish. Then we played base-ball so if you were batting you could get yourself a nice suntan.

'Compare that with the first day of pre-season under Jock. Bunny hops up the terracing, then with a partner on your back. I had to carry Greigy [John Greig], a real heavy boy, and guys were tumbling over the wall. Then compare that with the first day down at Gullane.

'Seven-thirty we left the stadium, jackets and ties as usual, picking up the Edinburgh-based lot at the east end of Princes Street where everyone – greedy footballers – grabbed an egg-and-sausage roll, not knowing what was ahead of them and Jock wasn't about to let on. I think I had a slice of toast ...'

Miller was astute, but he was also a teetotal fitness fanatic, not blessed with the greatest skill but compensating with a willingness to go the extra mile, even uphill, and when we talked at his Loch Lomond timeshare, he was just off the running machine:

'At Gullane we had to change into our kit in the car park in full view of the day trippers while Jock rammed poles into the sand. Running across the dunes was bloody hard and I was really fit. Jock kept hold of one pole and Derek Johnstone would get a whack: "Lift up yer fuckin' knees!"' *The Hill*'s Hendry would roar 'Eyes front!' and target the straggler: 'One of those shy lads, are you?' Wallace, a real soldier who'd once subsisted on monkey steaks, could be even more blunt.

'A young fellow, George Walker, collapsed,' continued Miller. 'He was given oxygen but then it was: "On yer fuckin' feet!"' There was a break for lunch, a nice hotel, with the shell-shocked players ascertaining the afternoon session would consist of 'just five-a-side' before diving into the grub. 'Greedy footballers – they all had minestrone soup, steak-and-kidney pie and rhubarb tart and custard. And Jock had tricked us: we were back on to the beach but this time it was Murder Hill.' Miller gazed up at the roof of his conservatory to illustrate the gradient; sand dancing in the style of music-hall favourites Wilson, Keppel and Betty was going to be impossible. 'Sixteen times we had to horse up there. Another boy, Davie Armour, was sick and that set off a chain reaction. Some guys hated Jock's methods. Willie Henderson did two laps of Ibrox, called the manager a 'mad bastard', grabbed his clothes off the hook, hailed a taxi, turned up the next day in the *Daily Record* sunbathing in Tenerife with his wife – and that was the finish of Willie. But I loved the mad bastard's methods and I loved Murder Hill.'

Do Rangers love a man in uniform? Er, is the Pope a non-Protestant? The men in royal blue have always been treated like squaddies with their smartness rigorously inspected. 'The turn-ups on your trousers could be no more than the width of three fingers,' confirmed Tommy McLean. 'The club were big on discipline: no golf, no nights out after Wednesday, wait for the green light above the manager's door before entering. And ten minutes to kick-off Jock would give us the fireman's hose, skooshing us with water to make sure we were alert. Then this strange oily lotion was rubbed on our scalps so we ran on to the pitch with our heads properly tingling.'

Murder Hill was another demonstration of Rangers' militarism. The enemy – Celtic, who'd won nine titles in a row – were finally defeated. How much of that was down to Wallace & Vomit? How much did the Gers view the world in a grain of sand? The dunes got Alex Miller and the rest fit, but no fitter than if they'd continued running up the terracing. There's a view that Murder Hill did more for the team's heads. The exertions were public, being witnessed by Mum, Dad and the weans from behind their windcheater, with the youngest putting down bucket and spade to ask, 'Why are these men crying?' – and they always made the news. Seeing themselves on TV and in the papers confronting an all too moveable object, the sand giving way beneath them, convinced the players they were the strongest, the toughest and the bravest in the land and football's equivalent of the Indian Army's Mountain Division, the absolute best at vertical warfare.

In short, that they were indomitable.

42

'The parka-clad schoolboy stampede across a quagmire'

TONY GREEN IN THE BLINK OF AN EYE

The humble macaroon bar has been anything but on these pages. And here's another mention of this epochal, emblematic sweetmeat, one linking it, however remotely, with nuclear science, the snorkel parka and George Best.

Tony Green dumped Bestie on his backside, something the majestic Northern Irishman did routinely to hapless opponents. Green was Newcastle United's little lucky charm, another from the Scottish production line of diminutive creatives, until injury finished him far too soon. As Magpies go, he was one for sorrow. Still revered on Tyneside, Geordies of a certain age make pilgrimages across the Pennines to knock on his door and pay their respects to a lost, bonnie talent.

Maybe, having only lasted 33 games, they expect to find a bitter man in the Lancashire market town of Poulton-le-Fylde. Nothing like, with Green having had an immensely fulfilling second life as a maths teacher.

Tell us about the time you bested Best, Bobby Charlton and Denis Law, the faithful implore, with the *Match of the Day* footage of the Green-inspired 1972 league win at Old Trafford being just about all that survives of his flickering playlet in the black and white.

He recounts that game, but will remind them that it immediately followed the club's most humiliating result, the FA Cup shock when little, non-league Hereford United sparked a parka-clad schoolboy stampede across a quagmire pitch.

Green had a good view of Ronnie Radford's siege-gun strike. 'I was right next to him,' he told me. 'It's gone into legend that I said: "Go on, shoot. You'll never score from here."' So there you have it: the most romantic goal in all football was inspired by a Scot, your actual McZelig.

There was an accidental aspect to the creation, by another Scot, of the macaroon bar. Confectioner John Justice Lees was striving for something chocolatey and when that was unsuccessful he decided to experiment with coconut. The macaroon bar was in good company here for in their respective labs Coca-Cola, Corn Flakes and crisps hadn't been part of the original plan either. Lees was a director at Albion Rovers when Green signed in 1964, a £7-a-week teenage tyro. When I called on him in Poulton-le-Fylde I'd been imagining there having been a Christmas gift of a box of 'Lees, Lees, more if you please' for every player, but Green couldn't confirm this.* 'I did, though, get a hurl in the company Rolls-Royce and there weren't many of them in Coatbridge. That was on the journey back from winning the Police Cup, a daft wee tournament for teams in and around Glasgow. We beat Celtic in the final and my brother John, a mad supporter, didn't speak to me for months afterwards.'

Green went from Cliftonhill to England's top flight, back when you could do that sort of thing, and from macaroon bars to Blackpool rock. Seasiders legend Stan Mortensen was the manager who'd announced to his chairman, 'I'm going up to watch Albion Rovers,' and was told: 'Just as long as you don't sign Tony Green – he's neither big enough nor good enough.' Green was, by his own admission, a 'wee skelf', but before too long on *Match of the Day*, in acclamation

---

* Willie Wallace was luckier. The Lisbon Lion began his career at Stenhousemuir whose Ochilview was next to the McCowan's toffee factory and Christmas would bring the team chewy treats, as would good results in the Scottish Cup.

of a couple of classy goals in the FA Cup, commentator Alan Weeks was raving: 'No wonder they say this boy is worth £100,000!'

He was elusive for defenders, also for crowds. Crocked for an entire year at Blackpool, 10,000 were desperate to see his comeback in the reserves. His brief international career was a pub quiz question with his first three games all featuring a Scotland own goal. He was slightly overawed by the company he was keeping on dark blue duty, recalling a Euros qualifier in Portugal: 'Willie Henderson, because he knew Eusebio, was invited up to the great man's villa. He came back with a crate of lovely wine and I said to him: "So will you be getting the Black Pearl through to Caldercruix now?"'

Then came Newcastle and, not much later, the smashed knee which forced him to quit at 25. 'When my manager, Joe Harvey, found out I wouldn't play again he took it very badly. I had to console him despite me being the one who was knackered.' What next? The three Green boys were different: John had been a beekeeper and a male nurse – the 'brainiest' one, apparently, which must be saying something because the other brother, Thomas, was a nuclear scientist. Their docker father, denied the opportunity himself, had been determined his sons would all go to university, and at Paisley Green had studied maths. So he brushed up on his algebra and geometry and ended up teaching for 30 years.

He joked that while Thomas in retirement was determined to get to the bottom of calculus, the study of continuous change, perhaps he should be devoting himself to infinitesimals – the number of coconut flecks produced annually by the Lees empire, still going strong. Of being a teacher he said: 'The satisfaction of helping kids crack a subject that had scared them was huge. I absolutely loved that job, so much so that I almost forgot I was ever a footballer.'

Others, though, won't let him. 'It's very humbling that I'm remembered because my time at Newcastle was the blink of an eye. When I go back to the city I can get quite emotional because the love from the fans can be overwhelming. Once this young lad stopped me for a photo. "I never saw you play," he said, "but you were my dad's favourite. Every new signing he'll still go: Not bad – but not as good as Tony Green." The last time I was there my cabbie kept turning round because he wanted to see my reaction to film on his phone of me leaving Bestie in a heap. He said: "For a change, George was the one left with twisted blood." But this guy very nearly drove us right over the Tyne Bridge.'

43

'This yellow 2CV screeched to a halt and out tumbled Mick Jagger'

GEORGE McCLUSKEY ATTEMPTS TO CHANGE THE COURSE OF ROCK MUSIC HISTORY

Footballers with excellent* taste in popular music would make a very small book. They may not even be able to fill one of the blank pages left for notes at the back of the *Wee Red Book*.**

Charlie Nicholas would doubtless seek inclusion after scoffing at his Celtic team-mates of the 1980s for falling for the blousy balladeering of podgy, Play-Doh-nosed Billy Joel – and when challenged to nominate his favourite pop act would extend his hands in a display of jodhpurs, sandals, Bedouin scarf, geometric jacket, isometric haircut, all enshrouded in a Sturmbannführer leather coat, and say: 'Isn't it obvious? Der Spands.'

Spandau Ballet. Superior to Chick Nick's ears, risible to yours and mine. This was the band with the singing foghorn, and so boomy

---

* 'Excellent' may be subjective, but my Little Feat will always beat your Little Mix, my Oneohtrix Point Never your One Direction.

** The pre-internet fixtures guide, published by Glasgow's *Evening Times* and small enough to fit in the breast pocket of a skinhead's Crombie. Not to be confused with Chairman Mao's *Little Red Book*. The latter's advice included: 'In waking a tiger, use a long stick.' Undoubtedly useful but not vital, like knowing when your team were playing Partick Thistle away.

and doomy was vocalist Tony Hadley that were he a real maritime alert, jaggy outcrops would be almost inviting. This was the band with the saxophonist who seemed to know just three notes. The band who sang about the smell of books when they burn and finding it so hard to write the next line, then rhymed 'diplomat' with 'laundromat'.

But one of those derided Parkhead team-mates bravely tried to change the course of music history. He ultimately failed, but it was a valorous act, which might have saved Rod Stewart from his personal fashion disaster – the LA-period horrors of leopard-print leggings and lemon visor – and some dreadful lyrics of his own, 'You're Celtic, United ... spread your wings and let me come inside' being uppermost.

In 1976 George McCluskey was among the cream of Scottish footballing youth who with the wee national team had just won through to the final of the prestigious Tournoi Juniors Under-18 de Cannes. The French resort's film festival was in full swing which could have added an extra layer of intimidating glamour for this Lanarkshire lad on his very first trip abroad. As it turned out, nothing like.

'The night before the final we'd had dinner but the lads were still hungry,' explained McCluskey, 'so myself and Rab Hannah formed an escape committee. We sneaked out of our hotel in search of some grub and stumbled across this wee place selling these big round things out of a window. But we'd never eaten pizzas before and so were struggling with the menu. Suddenly this yellow 2CV screeched to a halt beside us and out tumbled Mick Jagger. Three or four security guys followed him and I don't know how they all fitted in such a totty wee car. Then out came Ronnie Wood.

'Ronnie was great, asked us where we were from and how the football was going. We were having a good crack and that was when this toerag told the famous guitarist he'd made a terrible mistake joining the Stones and really he should have stayed with the Faces.'

Well, you would, wouldn't you? The Stones were a global entertainment behemoth, the Faces were a rock 'n' roll band, true to the original spirit. The Stones were corporate, the Faces were hedonistic. The Stones were establishment, the Faces were a glorious rabble. The Stones travelled by separate planes, the Faces piled up the back of the happy bus, no need for all those heavies. The Stones were in it for the money, the Faces for the parties. At least Stewart liked football and, er, model trains – what interested Jagger beyond making yet more money? Jagger may have defined rock frontmanship for the modern age but he'd become a parody of himself. Now Wood was going to have to stand behind him every night while he performed. To paraphrase Winston Smith, tragic hero of George Orwell's *Nineteen Eighty-four*: if you wanted a picture of the future, imagine a skinny, hollowed-out, satin-clad arse wiggling in a human face – forever.

'I kept asking Ronnie where Rod was,' added McCluskey. "I don't know," he said, "maybe LA?" I persisted with this line of enquiry for several minutes. Eventually he said: "Listen, George, I've just joined the best rock 'n' roll band in the world and you want me to get back with Rod. I love what you're saying but I don't think so!"'

People are much closer to celebrities now, or think they are, and some extremely ordinary folk even think they're celebrities themselves. In 1976 it was a bold thing to march straight up to a superstar and question his latest career move. McCluskey, though, was indomitable.

He would achieve his own fame as a dead-eyed striker with a hard, low, unerring finish in the corner of the net. But, while Celtic also had the aforementioned Charlie Nicholas and Frank McGarvey, George was invariably the one who started on the bench. Maybe the other two were the Stones, though, and he was the Faces, the cooler and more discerning choice.

That night in Cannes he parted on good terms with his new best rock-star mate. 'Ronnie invited me and Rab back to a party at the Stones' château and I've often wondered if that would have been the swally to end all swallies.' Anita Pallenberg? Marianne Faithfull? Other gorgeous muses lying around in not many clothes? 'I think we would have been out of our depth. Aye, by about 20,000 leagues. So like good boys we said: "Sorry, pal, but the team's pizzas are getting cold."'

44

'Impassive, inscrutable, inviolable, unbuyable'

THE HALF-TIME
SCOREBOARD OPERATOR

Oh yes, you know what's happening everywhere. You're connected to rolling football news and there's nothing about a hectic day of games that you miss – not a goal, a result, or a chunk of contextualising dynamite which doesn't just sum up a match but defines an epoch and explains the meaning of life, all of this coming fast and furious from the intellectual powerhouse radio screecher known as Biscuits.*

Your smartphone provides and lucky you. But we who subsisted on the most basic of info in comparison did not feel self-consciously small while we were present at one game and wondering what was happening in other games. You see, we had the half-time scoreboard.

The half-time scoreboard did what it said on the tin: provided midway-point progress on the rest of the Scottish card. In some cases it was a very big tin: a metal box of double-decker bus dimensions propped up on stilts. If you're looking for a comparison between then and now – how technological advancement has trimmed the size of things right down – then scoreboard to phone is a good one.

Such ostentation! Was the scoreboard invented by the Romans?

* *Sportsound* player-turned-pundit Allan Preston

Maybe the Egyptians, for it was a single-use monolith and its closest relative from history could have been the pyramid. Both involved large, elaborate construction for just one man: a pharaoh (deceased) or a stadium orderly with a bag of numbers and letters. But around ten to four on a Saturday afternoon, what drama the scoreboard provided!

What ceremony too. After the players had left the park for their break, the orderly and his bag would emerge from the tunnel. In my memory, the bag was made of hessian and resembled a satchel an artist might carry, but I may be over-romanticising the half-time scoreboard.

The orderly would walk round the pitch perimeter, impassive, inscrutable, inviolable, unbuyable. You could not read anything into his expression, and certainly not the score in Hearts' tricky away fixture at Dumbarton the Saturday after they'd lost the Edinburgh derby 7–0. And shouting at him to disclose it was futile. He was going into the box, and then and only then would the big reveal happen.

Easter Road boasted a fine scoreboard in a corner of the ground halfway up the terracing, which meant a journey of some conspicuousness for the operative. Fans would tease him with a slow-walk tune ('Do Not Forsake Me, Oh My Darling', the soundtrack to Gary Cooper's *High Noon*) or try to get him to speed up by na-na-na-ing the Benny Hill theme. If this annoyed or amused him, he didn't show it.

The letters and numbers brought the scores in code. Did we need Alan Turing-level cryptanalyst skills from a life burrowed in Bletchley Park to crack it? No, not really. A copy of the match programme sufficed and there would be a beautiful moment as the crowd as one turned to the page listing each fixture alongside a letter, looking for all the world like a church congregation leafing through their hymn books for the next psalm.

While we were being solemn and dutiful the scoreboard functionary was, incredibly, anticipating the mechanics of Bruce Forsyth's *Play Your Cards Right*, a full ten years before the emergence of the

Dolly Dealers. After first placing the letters on the big rack forming the front of the scoreboard – A for Aberdeen vs St Johnstone, B for Ayr United vs Dunfermline Athletic and so on – he would then pick up the required numbers.

But he didn't do this right away. There would be a pause which might have been theatrical or possibly teasing, maybe even sadistic – although it could also have been because of a bad phone line to some of the other grounds. The delay was sufficient for an anxious, hyperactive young mind to ponder all sorts of questions about the scoreboard man and his job.

Was it like being in charge of a lighthouse? Or maybe Thunderbird 5, the lonely space station hovering far above the world and still on duty while the other Tracy brothers back from their missions got to unwind with cocktails on the roof of International Rescue in turtleneck jumpers and medallions?

Did the operative have a kettle in there, a well-thumbed tale of the Wild West by J.T. Edson or a *Men Only* calendar on the back wall? Was his silent, solitary life replicated at home with no wife, no kids and just a cat called Brian Peter George St John le Baptiste de la Salle Thumper?

No matter, the great moment had arrived. What he'd waited all week and all of the first half for. Airdrie 0 would go up ... (What will it be? What will it be?) ... Dundee 0. (Oh well.) Next: Falkirk 0 ... East Fife 0. (Obviously another rip-roaring affair.)

It was home teams first unless the operative could have some fun with the state of play at, say, Ibrox when he might have given us Arbroath 1 ... before confirmation that Rangers had in fact banged in four. Groans and cheers greeted this little presentation, a modest ritual which over the course of the games' 15-minute interregnum would be challenged – but never bettered – by dance displays, tumbling demonstrations, police dog gymkhanas, junior penalty shoot-outs, keepy-uppy clowns, folkie strummers, raffle-drawing legends and much fancier electronic scoreboards flashing up personal greetings, an early intimation of the demise of traditional reserve.

(Soon, we would all be photographing ourselves ten times a day and everyone would be a star.)

On 23 October 1971, that was when the scoreboard guys became stars. Like Transit-bumping, toilet-playing heavy rockers with a dreary repertoire suddenly being gifted 'Smoke on the Water' to call their own, the operatives came off the phone from the Scottish League Cup final at Hampden and couldn't believe what they'd just been told. Celtic 0 … Partick Thistle 4. Are you sure? And we're allowed to make that public?

At Easter Road and doubtless every other ground there was a collective gasp ('The fool's got it wrong! … He's taken a funny turn!') Then came widespread jeering ('He's having a heart attack! … He's drunk!'). Laughter followed ('He's fallen out with the club! … He's been told his services are no longer required and for a big fuck-you he's dreamed up the maddest, wrongest half-time despatch there could ever be!') And finally, when the score wasn't corrected and it stayed right there on the board – astonishing, unyielding, indomitable – great roars of delight.

45

'Casey Kasem ripped him off,
copied his ironed hair'

WE WANT ARTHUR!
WE WANT ARTHUR!

'Come on, come on! This has got to be the last one!'

We've had *Casper the Friendly Ghost* which when you think about it is a contradiction in terms, like Gervaise the Metrosexual Hitman or Blaise the Non-Binary Steam Hammer Operator or Sasha the No Holds Barred, Full Contact, Ultimate Fighting World Champion Whose Walk-On Music is a Steps Megamix.

We've had *Spooky*, Casper's supposedly psychotic cousin, dangerous on account of his ill-fitting bowler hat, which in this country signifies 'civil servant', a harassed governmental fluffer, a Cyrano de Bergerac for politicians, buffing up their speeches for power-station openings. We've had *Tweetie Pie* and … go on, you stupid cat, stick him in a rye-bread sandwich and for once bite down on his silly twig legs!

Okay, I'm ten years old. I don't yet know what metrosexual, non-binary and the rest mean – no one does and won't for three decades. But I know this: *Glen Michael's Cartoon Cavalcade* is causing my teeth to curl and my fillings to pop and it's high time I was watching *Scotsport*.

'Get this rubbish off!' I scream and my little brother, until this moment so admiring, so trusting, looks at me with eyes full of hurt.

It's as if I've told him that, sorry, chum, we're not actually related. B-b-b-but, he sobs, I thought you liked *Cavalcade*? I thought we watched it together every Sunday afternoon sprawled on this strangely psychedelic rug in front of the three-bar electric fire with our macaroon bars, all snug and safe and hewn from the same rock?

The bond between us is broken. I'm moving on. The short-sighted oldster, the jet-propelled mouse, the stammering pig – I'm finished with all of them and their one-trick, one-note, one-dimensional story-lines. And I'm certainly finished with Michael.

The man wears pullovers of a pattern which, if you were feeling charitable, you might call 'busy'. You could also say: 'Casey "Top 40" Kasem ripped him off, copied his ironed hair too.' Or you might enquire: 'Which disturbed child drew these strange squiggles and have social services inspected them?' But we were all disturbed children during the Michael tyranny and our negligent parents didn't think it odd or even slightly creepy that the man talked to a lamp (and, bloody hell, the lamp talked back).

Everyone's favourite uncle? No, my favourite uncle lived on top of a goods line so when a train passed, the radiogram needle scratched his Semprini and he'd shake an angry fist at the rumbling load of ball bearings or slurry. He had a glass eye which fell into the kitchen sink, only to reappear later, leering every now and again from the plughole as if some kind of B-movie cyclops drain monster was down there – and once causing his wife, my auntie, to drop the pot of congealed semolina she was about to dump on the tinned tangerines (phew, close shave). During a family fireworks party a jumping jack leapt into his jacket pocket, setting him mildly ablaze, his elaborate leaping being the funniest moment of my life until that point. My favourite uncle was a Hearts fan who bought his *Daily Express* from the corner shop owned by retired Tynecastle winger Johnny Hamilton, with the latter's embellished yarns of great goals and stirring victories receiving further embroidery before they reached me.

Michael on the other hand refused to acknowledge football's existence. With stunningly casual sadism, he liked to make the *Scotsport* massive wait for its highlights fix. He'd taunt us with another three and a half minutes of crude animation, almost all of it coming with Brooklyn wise-guy accents. He'd tease us by bringing the biff-bam to a juddering halt then stepping into the action. This would raise our hopes. Was he about to denounce all cartooning as junk, confess to a life wasted in its curation? Was he about to go mad on air, like Peter Finch would do in the film *Network*, rant about the rubbishness of modern life and make to jump from a window which in his case would be a cartoon window, pretending to splat on to the pavement, or sidewalk, far below?

No, he was reminding us he used to be an actor, a pansticky board-treader, a mouth-agape thesp. Look at the fool, confronting the fourth wall in cream slacks and cream socks! These clunky, contrived interventions seemed to be Michael showing off to every director who deemed him not quite right for the dashing hero, the lead role – instead offering him the part of 'Muttering Villager No. 4'.

Come on, come on, it must be time for *Scotsport* now! What? Nooo! Here's *Abercrombie the Zombie* ... here's *Zippy Zephyr* ... here's *Honey Halfwitch* ... here's *Swifty and Shorty* ... and, crikey, here's *Pepé Le Pew*,* the satyromaniac skunk who repeatedly stalked, chased, groped and molested a cat called Penelope. In 2021, 76 years after the cartoon's first appearance, *The New York Times* was still lambasting its creators for 'normalising rape culture'. Me, I didn't find *Pepé Le Pew* funny. I didn't find any of *Cavalcade* funny. I wanted *Scotsport*. 'Yeah,' said my brother, scrunching up his macaroon wrapper and chucking it at the screen, seeing the light at last as the chubby galoot in tan slip-ons made out like he was Spiderman's best mate. 'Gerroff.'

---

* To be fair to Michael he would later ban Pepé from spraying his sleaze over *Cavalcade*, although here we might have had issues with the emperor thumb ruling over which cartoons we were permitted to watch, even when we didn't want to watch any.

46

'Like a penny banger exploding in a cast-iron dustbin'

ARCHIE GEMMILL
AND THE BEST OF US

It was 1978, the wedding of my school friend Hooky, and I was wondering: 'Who just threw *The Magic Boomerang*?'

Like in the TV show, everyone had stopped what they were supposed to be doing at that precise moment. Hooky and his bride Olive were not at the end of the receiving line welcoming their guests. The happy couple's parents were not celebrating with friends and relations over preprandial bubbly. The best man was not pacing a corridor, panicking over his speech.

The Magic Boomerang was a kids' adventure series from Australia. The action would be frozen, everyone else stock-still so the young hero could foil crime – the bendy stick's time in the air being sufficient for him to, for instance, arrange barrels as obstacles to scupper cattle rustlers. In this hotel, five televisions on stands were wheeled into the suite. Two hundred people had been set a trap, only they didn't know it yet. Scotland were beginning their World Cup adventure in Argentina and the nuptials had been halted, to resume after the routine thrashing of Peru. What could possibly go wrong?

Everything. Scotland lost. Stunned silence. The joyful mood could not be retrieved and the wedding turned into a wake. I don't know why Hooky agreed to the interruption as he didn't follow football –

he was a King Crimson fan. But then Ally MacLeod's Pied Piper act had the whole country marching smartly behind. After the party fizzled out, I walked home through town with Bob, a Mahavishnu Orchestra fan who suddenly had an opinion about our best midfield.

The streets were angry. Nearly murderous. We daren't have caught anyone's eye, such was the desire to fight, though whether any of these malcontents could have swung a punch was highly debatable. Every single one was a careering drunk, staggering and raging and staggering some more.

Fast-forward a week when a player in dark blue replicated the moves of the guys Bob and I dodged following the Peru game. After the dismal draw with Iran, Scotland needed to beat Holland by three goals. Archie Gemmill very nearly made the impossible happen. By fooling the total football aristocrats into believing he was blootered.

How very Scottish, you might think, to take a word like 'miraculous' – *Oxford Dictionary* meaning: 'Of the nature of a miracle, supernatural' – and see the potential for an alternative use. Gemmill's second goal in Mendoza at the culmination of an insane dribble was miraculous. But, in his weeble-wobble weaving, *he* was miraculous.

'I dinnae drink,' Gemmill said firmly when I managed to drag him away from his garden in Derby. 'Or at least I didnae then. I grew up in Paisley's Ferguslie Park and saw so many folk get in a terrible state with the booze. I decided: "Nah, not for me."

'But, to be honest with you, I don't know what I was doing when I scored that goal. I've been asked about it a million times so maybe I should have a better answer by now, but I'm afraid I don't.'

Gemmill is possibly, of all the footballers I've met, the least likely to ever embellish a yarn. Some of his have been Laurence Llewelyn-Bowen-ed* – spray-painted with gold leaf for the complete baroque overload – but not by him.

One such was Brian Clough being so desperate to sign him for Derby County that when talks at the player's house reached impasse,

---

* LLB, the un-shy and non-retiring host of makeover show *Changing Rooms*.

Old Big 'ead was all set to sleep in his car, parked outside. That bit is true but Cloughie, invited inside by Gemmill's wife, did not then remove his shoes and kip by the fire; he was offered the spare room. He did not greet Gemmill the next morning in his Y-fronts and nor did he cook the eggs. The deal, though, would be concluded.

But if he won't over-egg the miraculousness of Mendoza then maybe we will have to do this. For instance, how, collecting the ball just outside the Dutch box, he seemed to be acting out the Billy Connolly gag about a valiant attempt at forward motion despite being in a high state of over-refreshedness: one foot planted while the other jabbed at various points on the ground like a compass being twirled round its arc.

Then, having opted for the direction of travel, it was as if the wee sozzled guy embarked on a confident zigzag to the bar or on to the dance floor or across the road with a swerving gait in pursuit of the last bus home.

Gemmill was like Dancer in Peter McDougall's 'Play for Today' *Just a Boys' Game*, bunking off work and escaping domestic duty with an erratic, exuberant gallop to go on the bevvy with his mates at ten in the morning. But, you know, we can end the connotations with alcohol right there ...

In *Gregory's Girl*, the hero dithers and dauners and delays his arrival at school with an elaborate amble across the red-ash sports field. Bill Forsyth's film came two years after Argentina and that scene was surely inspired by Gemmill.

Gregory, as played by John Gordon Sinclair, and Dancer (Ken Hutchison) are big, long drinks of water; Gemmill is short, compact, Cagneyesque.

Being one of the little guys – a Caledonian classic – was no impediment in a career of glittering prizes with Derby and, later under Clough, no through-the-night lobbying needed this time, Nottingham Forest.

Young Gemmill, son of a slater and a cleaner, spoiled rotten as an only child, grew to the undizzy height of 5ft 5ins and then stopped.

He can't remember if any boys' coach ever said to him, 'Sorry, son, you're too wee,' but he wouldn't have listened anyway. Size for him and a few others on these pages wasn't everything. The trick, even if the height disadvantage made him nervous or worried, was never to show it.

Gemmill doesn't watch football now and doesn't recognise midfielders any more. 'It's pass, pass, pass but most of them are bloody pointless,' he sighed. 'Anyone can shuffle the ball across the park behind halfway – it means damn all.'

A comparison can be made with politics. The contemporary midfield man is like the junior minister who's always fudging and flimflamming, ducking the tough questions, hiding behind his boss, preferring to wait for the official report some time hence. Gemmill in '78 fronted up for the Progressive Party and he had to do this.

Scotland, according to Rod Stewart, were in 'Endsville'. Drugs had piled shame on humiliation but the banned Willie Johnston might have been fortunate, being able to slip back home early. What kind of welcoming party was lying in wait for the official team plane after the inevitable exit from the World Cup and how many from that vengeful wedding night would be at Prestwick Airport?

'If any player who scores a goal tells you how they did it, what they were thinking, how time stood still and that sort of rubbish, then they're lying,' added Gemmill. 'Mine just happened, goodness knows how.'

Well, I think on this occasion time did stop. The Dutch defenders became statues, like cattle thieves rooted to the spot. Gemmill hurled the magic boomerang, and as it spun – and as he jinked and bobbed with those chunky legs and busy arms – a nation forgot they'd ever been banished to Endsville and began to fantasise about 'Dreamland'.

Regarding the goal, how very Scottish for there to be this jewel – with diamonds running down the scorer's sleeves – amid the slurry. How very Scottish, as Don Masson confessed to me, for some players sitting in the stand to silently mouth, 'Christ, Archie, what the hell are you doing?' because they wanted the World Cup to be over, the nightmare of Argentina to end. And how very Scottish for that boomerang bliss to last just three minutes before Holland scored to kill the game.

Gemmill's zany meander has been marked out on the floor of the Scottish Football Museum underneath Hampden, rather like how the police would delineate a crime location. The goal has been commemorated in a shagging scene in the *Trainspotting* movie and turned into a dance by the English National Ballet but, really, I don't think I've mentioned enough how beautiful it was.

A Borders weaver, working in fiendishly intricate patterns, would have admired the goal. A Kincardineshire fisherman would have smiled at the similarity with the swishing of his nets as he dried them. The Associates' Billy MacKenzie with that swooping and soaring voice would have loved the goal. So would the artist John Bellany with his swooping and soaring paintbrush. So would the writer Alasdair Gray, a specialist in magical fabulism. And R.D. Laing, psychiatrist of the Swinging Sixties counterculture, might have reasoned: 'I don't remember dropping any acid so what Archie did just there must have been the wildest and craziest dream.'

I did not blurt any of this to Gemmill. I did not tell him that when he turned away to celebrate his goal, fist pumping, he resembled a wee holy terror making good his escape after setting off a penny banger in an empty cast-iron dustbin in the doorway of a big posh house. If I had, he probably would have sent me away, minus any extended, Cloughie-style hospitality. He was insistent that it was 'just a goal'. In the grander scheme of the World Cup, it 'didnae matter'.

But in the grander scheme of Scottish culture, history, identity, ingenuity, swagger and never say die, it was everything. Truly, it was the best of us.